The Transformed Library

ALA Editions purchases fund advocacy, awareness, and accreditation programs for library professionals worldwide.

THE TRANSFORMED LIBRARY

E-Books, Expertise, and Evolution

Jeannette
WOODWARD

An imprint of the American Library Association • Chicago • 2013

Jeannette Woodward is a principal of Wind River Library and Nonprofit Consulting. After a career in academic library administration, most recently as assistant director of the David Adamany Library at Wayne State University, she began a second career in public libraries as the director of the Fremont County Library System in the foothills of the Wind River Mountains of Wyoming. Woodward is the author of several books, including *A Librarian's Guide to an Uncertain Job Market* (2011), *Countdown to a New Library*, 2nd ed. (2010), *Creating the Customer-Driven Academic Library* (2008), *Creating the Customer-Driven Library: Building on the Bookstore Model* (2005), and *Countdown to a New Library: Managing the Building Project* (2000). Woodward holds a master's degree in library and information science from Rutgers University, with doctoral study at the University of Texas at Austin.

• • •

Printed in the United States of America

17 16 15 14 13   5 4 3 2 1

Extensive effort has gone into ensuring the reliability of the information in this book; however, the publisher makes no warranty, express or implied, with respect to the material contained herein.

ISBNs: 978-0-8389-1164-8 (paper); 978-0-8389-9628-7 (PDF); 978-0-8389-9629-4 (ePub); 978-0-8389-9630-0 (Kindle). For more information on digital formats, visit the ALA Store at alastore.ala.org and select eEditions.

Library of Congress Cataloging-in-Publication Data

Woodward, Jeannette A.
  The transformed library : e-books, expertise, and evolution / Jeannette Woodward.
    p. cm
  Includes bibliographical references and index.
  ISBN 978-0-8389-1164-8
  1. Libraries—Aims and objectives.   2. Libraries—Forecasting.   3. Libraries and electronic publishing.   4. Libraries—Information technology.   5. Libraries and the Internet.   6. Librarians—Effect of technological innovations on.   7. Library science—Philosophy.   8. Libraries and society.
  I. Title.
  Z678.W675 2013
  020—dc23   2012023767

Cover design by Kirstin Krutsch.
Book design by Adrianna Sutton using Cartier and Bonveno typefaces.

♾ This paper meets the requirements of ANSI/NISO Z39.48-1992 (Permanence of Paper).

To my family: Laura, Chris, Lowell, John, and David, with all my love

CONTENTS

INTRODUCTION

Looking back on the first decade of the twenty-first century, we can't be blamed for feeling somewhat depressed about our libraries and the situation they are facing. During a decade that will always be known for the most dramatic economic downturn since the Great Depression, libraries have fared badly. On the one hand, library budgets have been slashed and some libraries have disappeared in a puff of smoke or a blot of red ink. On the other hand, pundits loudly announce the death of libraries. All the materials that libraries select and catalog and house and lend will soon be digitally available, they say, making libraries as extinct as the dodo.

THE DIGITAL TRANSITION

Is this true, we wonder? What else could possibly provide libraries with a reason for being if not these information-bearing objects? Think of the library science courses, the conferences, the workshops, the manuals, the billions or perhaps trillions of staff hours that have been devoted to the care of library materials. Those of us in denial respond that no e-reader will ever replace the comfy, cozy, tactile experience of paper and ink, but is this merely wishful thinking? If digital files do replace most physical media, can libraries and librarians simply regroup, restock their virtual shelves with virtual media, and continue to play much the same role as in years gone by? Has the dismal economy clouded our vision and made us view the future through unnecessarily dark lenses? On the other hand, is the financial crisis actually propelling libraries toward a bleak future? Such speculations inevitably lead to musings about our profession and the possibility that we will be outsourced or become an extinct species. This book is intended to provide a balanced assessment of the situation that confronts both libraries and information professionals. It will present some possible future scenarios, moving beyond rosy visions of patrons lovingly embracing handsome examples of the printer's art and Fahrenheit 451-spawned, apocalyptic nightmares of a world without libraries.

DEFINING THE LIBRARY

Although it may at first seem unnecessary, I'll need to establish some boundaries around my subject matter, and the best way to do that is to define clearly what I mean by a library. Until fairly recently, the meaning of the term was clear and unequivocal. Libraries were usually buildings filled with printed materials and a trained staff to assist patrons using those materials. Libraries were maintained by local governments, academic institutions, or nonprofits. Special libraries were a little different, but in general the definition was quite simple. More recently, libraries added multimedia formats to their collections and then digital materials that occupied no physical space. These materials were available on the library's computers and on the library's website, so they were rather easily absorbed into the definition.

Then digital libraries were created. The library and information science (LIS) professionals and technical staff responsible for them were usually housed in the library building. Their role consisted largely of converting certain significant and perhaps inaccessible library-owned materials to digital formats and organizing them for more effective access. Such materials were usually included in the library's online catalog, and so there was little question that the digital library was an extension of the traditional library, even though its collection did not occupy space in the library stacks.

NEW DEFINITIONS

For many years, libraries had little competition when it came to organizing and providing access to materials. However, as information, especially digital information, grew rapidly in value, for-profit businesses found that they could make money providing services that were once the exclusive province of libraries. While libraries were slowly expanding their virtual presence, other organizations like Google were taking giant leaps, using their vast financial assets to digitize the world's storehouse of books and other information resources. Such organizations prefer their output to be viewed as libraries because we have a solid reputation for altruism and public service. Subscription database vendors also like the term. Thus, the term *library* became flexible, often including the output of commercial businesses.

Nonprofit organizations also began taking part in library-like activities. For example, groups of scientists got together to create preprint servers intended to get around the ponderous, time-consuming requirements of peer-reviewed journals. Preprints allow scientists to know what their peers are doing long before they receive the official stamp of approval that journal publication represents. Researchers in other fields have developed similar collections, organized in ways that sound very familiar to librarians. They intend to meet the information needs of their users just as libraries exist to meet similar information needs. In other words, once we accept the premise that digital libraries, which developed under the umbrella of traditional libraries, meet our definition of a library, it's hard to know where to stop.

For the purpose of this book, however, I've settled on a rather restrictive definition. I am a librarian writing for others who see themselves as librarians, whether digital or traditional. Although we may take on other titles, we view ourselves as direct descendents of Ranganathan and Melvil Dewey. The future well-being of preprint servers is important to many, but I'm going to limit my definition so as to exclude projects that arise totally outside the traditional brick-and-mortar library. I am also going to exclude the products of for-profit corporate entities like Google that may be seen as repackaging information resources to enhance their profitability. Even though in making millions of public domain works available to millions of people, Google has in a sense "out-libraryed" any library, Google nevertheless exists for the purpose of making money. In fact, as will later become evident, it remains to be seen whether such enterprises pose future challenges and even dangers to libraries or whether partnerships will arise that benefit all parties.

THE RECOGNIZABLE LIBRARY

Perhaps I should also specify that according to the definition I will be using, a library must be recognizable as such to the public. In other words, it must meet their definition as well as mine. As I read futurist books and articles about libraries, I sometimes come across visions that are exciting, but they describe something that has evolved into an organization or institution today's library users would not recognize. Of course, our definitions will become increasingly more flexible as we move into the future. Librarians pursuing their profession in the 1920s or '30s might not recognize today's library but as we look back, we can see a gradual evolution. There has been a steady, logical transition from then to now. The library's mission and goals are largely unchanged, although they have been impacted by changes in both technology and society. The visions I am talking about may well be realized in the future, but something very unexpected will need to happen. Some radical shift will need to occur.

PREDICTING CHANGE

Although in hindsight we can see that libraries have developed much as one might expect them to, considering the changing environment, we must remember that we cannot turn our gaze toward the future with the same success. The patterns we see so clearly when we look back do not provide much insight into tomorrow's innovations and institutions. Again and again pundits have been wrong when predicting how computers will change human experience. The Jetsons' jet packs never made it to prime time, and what futurist ever predicted the culture-altering phenomenon of e-books?

Though librarians have coped well when confronted with change, they have proven to be no more successful than anyone else at predicting it. Nevertheless, we who have spent years identifying and anticipating customers' needs should be able to avoid most of the obvious errors of crystal ball gazing. It may be helpful to look at our experience more carefully and see whether we can discover any "intimations" of the future. Again and again, when we look at innovative library ideas and services that worked as compared to the failures, it appears that a keen knowledge of human nature was at the core of the successes. Knowing what people need is certainly important, but knowing what they enjoy and what makes them feel comfortable is at least as important. I think as librarians, we missed the boat with social networking. We saw how the use of cell phones exploded, not merely as substitutes for landlines but as a source of companionship for people who didn't want to be alone. Text messaging provided an even more intimate presence. Texters could go on doing what they were doing, knowing there was a comforting message waiting from a friend.

RESPONDING TO CHANGE
Libraries have tended to observe these developments, but most have not really understood how they relate to libraries. For example, some libraries have developed vital presences on Facebook and Google+, with hundreds or even thousands of friends actively seeking togetherness on the library site, but more typical Facebook sites look like posters or brochures. There's nothing alive about them. Such libraries fail to understand that for their Facebook presence to be successful, it must be an ongoing conversation. There must truly be a sense of connection between the library's "friends" and their library.

CHANGING INFORMATION SOURCES
Before moving on to the first chapter, I'd like to share some personal thoughts about the Internet and the future of libraries. Years ago, when I first began using the Internet for my own research, I very rarely strayed from the library's subscription databases. Gradually, I became bolder and my first milestone was perhaps the realization that I was using Wikipedia for background information far more often than the revered *Britannica*. If a fact is important, I continue to double-check more traditional sources, but I'm often astounded at the quality of Wikipedia articles. Other milestones followed as I discovered more and more valuable resources, often covered by Creative Commons license. The present book represents another milestone. In addition to interviewing many practicing librarians, I turned to library blogs to get a better sense of how librarians are feeling and how their libraries are changing.

What I found surprised me. Unlike many Internet blogs that are casual affairs, sometimes poorly written opportunities for spreading unreliable information, library blogs contain some of the most useful information available anywhere. They are well-written, factually accurate, and on the cutting edge of our discipline. I might have expected that librarians would write literate, grammatical prose, but I did not anticipate that in many cases, these professional blogs would be more insightful than articles found in "A"-list library journals. When I thought about it, however, it made perfect sense. As a group, librarians rank very high on IQ charts; they're technically savvy, read widely, and consequently tend to be good writers. The blog format provides the near-perfect opportunity for them to use their talents. While reading an especially thoughtful post, it occurred to me that blogs may be an invaluable library survival tool. They allow librarians in the trenches to share their experiences, thus discouraging one another from making wasteful mistakes, and spreading the word about successful projects. My blog discoveries served to reinforce my strong conviction that the future depends largely on us—in other words, on committed LIS professionals who are at the helm, steering libraries around rocky shoals into calmer waters.

1 GUTENBERG MEETS KINDLE

THE ARRIVAL OF DIGITAL BOOKS

A ny useful predictions concerning the future of libraries must take into consideration a plethora of issues. Nearly every change in both our economy and our society will inevitably be felt by the library. However, if we look back at the last thirty or so years of library evolution, the changes that immediately spring to mind have to do with technology. Computers have both eliminated and created library jobs. They have radically changed the way libraries function. That means that a realistic analysis of technology trends, including newly emerging technologies, is essential. The problem is that most futurists and other technology gurus have been notoriously inaccurate. Much or perhaps most of what they envisioned never happened, while breathtaking developments that completely altered the way we conduct our daily lives went unnoticed until they were fait accompli.

WHY FUTURISTS GET IT WRONG

Every once in a while, of course, someone gets it right. Alvin Toffler was spot on when, in 1980, he envisioned the electronic cottage where people could meet their personal needs and conduct successful businesses without leaving home. His insight was truly amazing considering that as he was writing *The Third Wave,* personal computers were little more than toys.[1] Technology in a typical household included only a television, record player, and single-line telephone. Yet for every futurist like Toffler who got it right, there must be dozens of dreamers who failed to understand key technical issues or the way human beings respond to new inventions. Take, for example, the world inhabited by that cartoon family, *The Jetsons.* We are not much closer to relying on "jet packs" for routine transportation than we were when the program first aired. Although the technology is available to lift human beings into the air and propel them from place to place, widespread use of such a technology would cause innumerable problems. Something may happen to make such a mode of transportation safe and efficient, but it is unlikely in the foreseeable future. Instead, society is under pressure to move from the transport of single individuals, an activity that consumes vast amounts of fossil fuel, to mass public transportation to accommodate our ever-growing urban population and conserve dwindling natural resources.

Similar mistakes were made by Paul Ehrlich. His book *The Population Bomb* predicted that by the end of the twentieth century, the human race would reproduce to the point of explosion, greatly exceeding available resources. Mass starvation would sweep the globe and civilization would come to a screeching halt. Many countries would collapse because of their inability to feed their citizens and would cease to exist. Although Ehrlich's failure was based on a number of incorrect assumptions, one of the most basic was assuming that human beings would go on exactly as they had in the past, failing to respond to the problems that confronted them. He did not take technological innovation into consideration or the possibility that an environmental movement could effect major change. Human beings adapt to their environment and that is how they survive. Just because events followed a particular pattern or blueprint in the past does not mean that they will continue to do so.

Anticipating Paradigm Shifts

Also consider the disconnect between IBM founder Thomas Watson and today's smartphone environment. A smartphone is actually a computer that doubles as a telephone and performs a variety of other functions. It would not exist if it had not been for the innovative work of Watson and other early computer scientists. However, Watson predicted that it would take no more than a few dozen computers to satisfy market demand. He envisioned only large corporations and research facilities having any need for them. Yet today, the average person has a computer in his pocket, another at home, and yet another at work. The same kind of myopia has been characteristic of most predictions, and it is not until the moment has almost arrived that most of us get a glimpse into the future. When and how do we become aware that our world has changed in a fundamental way? When do we first become conscious of those misty glimmers of the future that gradually become clear and detailed images? At what point does the totally improbable become the perfectly natural and we feel confident enough to plan our lives and our libraries around it?

A Personal Experience

Consider my own experience with the evolution of digital books. Sometime around 1995, I wrote an article about future libraries.[2] Computer users were surfing the Web with Netscape and Lycos, the forerunners of modern "web crawler" search engines. If you're an old-timer, you may remember that Magellan, Excite, AltaVista, and Infoseek soon followed. That was the digital world as I was then experiencing it. Even using those relatively primitive search engines, it was not hard to predict that library customers would soon lose patience with printed reference works. Once they became accustomed to typing a few words into a search box and immediately discovering dozens of articles and websites, they would be unwilling to spend hours poring over indexes printed in tiny type fonts.

Journal articles stored on CD-ROMs also made their appearance about that time, and though it was clunky to load and unload disks each time you needed another article, they were certainly more convenient than searching through dusty periodical stacks. It became clear from such developments that libraries would not long continue to maintain bound back runs of most newspapers and other periodicals. From there, it was not too big a stretch to imagine that digital versions of current magazines and newspapers might someday be available and fully searchable on the Internet.

What didn't make sense to me, however, was any sort of future for electronic books. If one were going to read a longer work from beginning to end, a task spread over at least several days, there seemed to be nothing comparable to the comfort and efficient design of the printed book. When I wrote about library design in 2000 in *Countdown to a New Library*,[3] I still felt much the same way. Project Gutenberg was speeding up production, and thanks to improved scanners and optical character recognition software, a number of e-books were widely available. However, this was surely a drop in the bucket compared to the millions of books housed in libraries. I cautioned my readers that the digital world was changing rapidly and some media were going the way of the duck-billed platypus, but it didn't appear that printed books were in any immediate danger.

E-Publishing Explodes

My thoughts continued to evolve but it was not until 2009, as I was editing the second edition of *Countdown to a New Library*,[4] that I had my "Aha!" experience. A group of librarians were having coffee. We had all attended a conference program and since it ended a little early, we decided to take a quick coffee break. Somehow the conversation turned to e-books and experiences with vendors. One of the men in the group admitted that he was looking for a cheap e-book service that would allow his library to appear up-to-date and high-tech but one that wouldn't cost a lot of money. "I just don't see it going very far, but it looks good for the library." Another librarian thought he should be more positive. "We've been lending e-books for a few years and they're pretty popular. Of course, they'll never replace print but they're fine for what they do." Then a third librarian chimed in with that comment so many of us have made: "No, nothing will ever replace the touch and smell of books. People will always want the real thing."

It was then that lightning flashed and the ground shook. My technology timetable was irrevocably altered and those years before e-books dominated the market shrank like a balloon that has lost its air. It wasn't that I had been blind to e-reader technology. When Amazon's Kindle arrived in 2007, I was fascinated by the electronic paper technology on which it was based. I had even purchased my first e-reader and loved it. Standing in a long supermarket line, I discovered I could reach into my pocket, pull out my reader, and go immediately to the page where I last stopped reading. I could remove myself from the irritating situation of standing in line, and as long as I reserved enough brain power to push my cart ahead, I could contentedly remain immersed in my mystery story.

Nostalgia for Printed Books

Getting back to my coffee klatch, I knew that I myself had said much the same thing about the touch and smell of printed books. I own way too many books and they occupy a ridiculously large amount of space in my home. A friend asked why I, a librarian, didn't just borrow my books from the library. I responded that libraries aren't open at 3:00 a.m. on sleepless nights when books are the best of companions. Neither is the library convenient if I merely want to look something up or reread a favorite poem. Thus, I find excuses for holding on to far too many books that I never quite finish or will never read again.

Looking around at the coffee drinkers (decaf actually), it struck me that most of us were about the same age, meaning what you might euphemistically call "mature." Printed books had been our companions since we first learned to read. Wasn't much of what I was hearing a combination of nostalgia and firmly entrenched habit? I remembered times when I was traveling alone and was forced to wait for hours in a grimy, impersonal airport enduring one long flight delay after another. The paperback I pulled from my purse was certainly not bound in leather and the smell of cheap paper was not especially appealing, but the finest first edition would not have given me any more comfort than that dog-eared old friend. Is there really any reason why readers won't turn to their e-books for the same comfort and reassurance? The answer, of course, is that touch and smell really have little bearing on how we choose most of the objects in our lives. Thinking back over the other negative comments voiced by the group, none were based on solid fact. Engaging in nostalgia can be an enjoyable pastime, but the future of the book will depend on more objective considerations.

HOW WE READ PRINTED TEXT

How do e-text and e-readers differ from printed books? To make any intelligent predictions about the future of printed books, we probably need to spend a little time understanding how our eyes see and our brains process printed characters. It turns out that the brain is very fussy. The brain objects when a block of text does not look like the blocks of text it has become accustomed to. Throughout history, loud objections have been raised with the arrival of each new media format. William Wordsworth's sister insisted he was damaging his mind reading the newspapers of the day. She was reacting to the new format of a large page on which multiple columns of text were placed side by side, thus creating a very disorienting experience for the reader. There may be nothing inherently better about the layout of a printed book, but the human brain has become accustomed to it.

If you think about a typical web page, it may seem as if the webmaster is deliberately trying to disorient the reader. Some lines of text contain twice the number of characters as a typical page in a printed book, making it nearly impossible for our eyes to scan the lines without losing our place. On the other hand, some columns are so narrow that a line consists of no more than three or four words and they may be contained in small boxes thrust in the middle of longer lines of text. Add to that the many ads that are positioned more prominently than the text we want to read and the brain naturally rebels. Because we are allowed no organized sense of the whole page, we don't know where to look first, so our reading becomes confused and out of sequence. In addition, there are constant distractions in what might be called the margins that encourage us to abandon the text we're reading and click on an appealing graphic or headline.

Viewing a Computer Monitor

Then there's the problem of the computer screen itself. Light from early computer monitors flickered so constantly that they were the cause of frequent headaches. More recently, reading has become easier as computer screens have improved. Users have also become more accustomed to them, their brains more readily accepting differences between computer text and printed text. However, people read more slowly on screen, often by as much as 20–30 percent. Tests of student comprehension also showed very significant loss compared to paper, but those differences have diminished in more recent studies.

Since reading on screen requires more effort, it can be more tiring. However, in the case of computer users who have been reading e-text for a number of years, the differences are not great and are noticeable only for difficult text. However, the ability to flip back and forth in a printed book aids substantially in comprehension, and the word-search capability usually provided by computer programs is not a very satisfactory substitute. Human brains have also become skilled at snapping pictures of how individual pages look and remembering where information appears on a page. Such memories are far from exact but they speed the process considerably.

Browsing

It is possible, however, that librarians place too much value on the advantages of browsing, both in books and among library stacks. It is likely that the precision of computer searching adds substantially to comprehension. Many of us have had the experience of pulling one book and then another from its shelf in the stacks, scanning a few pages, and then having a kind of "Eureka!" experience. Our active brains, coupled with the physical experience of browsing, produced a realization or connection that might not otherwise have occurred to us. However, Alan Liu, department chair and professor of English at the University of California, Santa Barbara, writes: "Show me one person who has made a serendipitous discovery while wandering the library stacks, and I will show you a thousand whose eyes glazed over at the sheer anomie, inefficiency, and meaninglessness of it all."[5]

On the other hand, the distractions associated with e-text may increase confusion. While one waits for a page to load, the mind wanders. If the wait is more than a few seconds, we have a tendency to click away from the text to check our e-mail or even look at the time. In tests of office workers using computers, it was discovered that they switched tasks approximately every three minutes and it took over twenty-three minutes for them to return to their tasks. Users are more likely to click away from less interesting to more interesting text, making it harder to concentrate on difficult material.

No Hard-Wiring

Maryanne Wolf is a faculty member in the Eliot-Pearson Department of Child Development at Tufts University. She believes that humans have no genetic predisposition to read. "Each young reader has to fashion an entirely new 'reading circuit' afresh every time. There is no one neat circuit just waiting to unfold . . . This 'open architecture' of the reading circuit makes the young reader's developing circuit malleable to what the medium (e.g., book, computer text, etc.) provides. And that, of course, is the problem. No one really knows the ultimate effects of immersion in digital media on the young developing brain. We do know a great deal, however, about the formation of the expert reading brain that most of us possess up to this point in history."[6]

Does this mean that we adults who developed brain circuitry to read printed books experience difficulties with digital text that children who learn to read on computers never experience? Could it be that in just a generation, we will see the end of printed books? Watching my three-year-old grandson read literally hundreds of children's books on his mother's Kindle Fire leads me to think so. I certainly could not read at age three. However, David Gelernter, professor of computer science at Yale University, doesn't agree. "All reading is not migrating to computer screens. So long as books are cheap, tough, easy to 'read' from outside (What kind of book is this? How long is it? Is this the one I was reading last week? Let's flip to the pictures), easy to mark up, rated for safe operation from beaches to polar wastes and—above all—beautiful, they will remain the best of all word-delivery vehicles."[7] He goes on to suggest integrating chips into books and not the other way around. That way he could make the book beep when he can't find it, search text online, and download updates. He suggests inserting a chip and battery into the binding to accomplish these tasks but when they fail to function, he can still read the book. One especially good point he makes is that technologists have decreed the disappearance of the book without bothering to understand it. They don't really understand the physical side of reading.

Nevertheless, the computer makes it possible to absorb information in entirely new ways that cannot be measured by traditional tests of speed or comprehension. For example, if you type a single term, the search function lets you move around an e-book so rapidly that you can get a sense for the entire work. You can follow a specific topic from page to page and chapter to chapter, using the search engine to restructure the book to meet your own needs and avoid wasting time on peripheral information. Hypertext even allows you to follow your own thoughts and questions, diverging from the somewhat "single-minded" linear outline of a book. Of course, hypertext can be viewed as yet another distraction, sending you off on different tangents that take you further and further away from the book you set out to read.

THE ARRIVAL OF THE E-READER

Although electronic gadgets specifically intended for reading text have been available for a number of years, it was not until Amazon introduced the Kindle that they began attracting a lot of public attention. Electronic readers specifically intended for reading book files have altered many of our assumptions about reading and the brain. E-readers like those marketed by Amazon, Sony, and Barnes & Noble share characteristics of both computer text and ink-imprinted paper. However, since they are a recent arrival, research on them is still in its infancy.

Anecdotal evidence suggests that e-readers are considerably more comfortable for reading lengthy works than computers, and many people read them as quickly as they do print formats. Screens are easier to read than computer monitors because electronic ink technology avoids problems like backlighting and flicker. Because readers can make type larger or smaller, e-text is sometimes easier to read than printed books. Browsing through multiple pages is somewhat awkward, and it can be annoying to wait for the page to turn. E-readers are much smaller and lighter than either computers or most hardback books, so they're comfortable to hold for long periods. Contrast can be a problem in low light but, of course, this is true for printed works as well. Illustrations are currently a weakness, and it seems that it will be quite a while before e-reader illustrations rival the brilliant images found in today's coffee-table books. However, most of the problems cited here appear to be "fixable." At this point in time, it seems that most e-book customers are enjoying their new readers "in addition to," not "instead of," their printed books.

Amazon Kindle

For several years, Kindles completely dominated the e-reader market. This was largely because Amazon had grown into such a huge online presence, calling itself the largest bookstore in the world. The Kindle itself was also extraordinarily user-friendly. It was designed to download new e-titles with a single click. From the beginning, Kindle had Wi-Fi capability, so there was no need to transfer files from computer to e-reader. 3G models followed so readers could purchase books anywhere at any time. A selection of free books kept readers coming back to the Kindle store, and free samples seduced customers with the potato-chip principle: once they'd sampled a title, they wanted more. Kindle was quickly joined by several other readers, each offering either a lower price or a feature that assured it at least a small chunk of the market. So many competitors emerged that Kindle prices dropped dramatically; currently the basic model is available for $79. Free Kindle software has made it possible for users to synchronize their e-books on any compatible device. The Kindle format is proprietary, however, and e-books are not compatible with other e-readers.

For a time, Amazon's dominant position appeared to be weakening as other brands like Barnes & Noble's Nook cut into its market share. However, the recent settlement of a lawsuit brought by the Justice Department against major publishers has strengthened Amazon's hand. The suit alleged that publishers were colluding to raise the price of e-books and prevent Amazon from selling them at bargain prices. High volume and aggressively low prices have been largely responsible for Amazon's success, so Amazon appears to be back in the driver's seat.

Sony Readers

It seems appropriate to give Sony's e-book reader, called the Reader, a bit more attention here, not because it is Amazon's strongest competitor but because the company has consistently courted libraries. As librarians, we can be forgiven for sometimes thinking that e-book publishers and distributors are determined to shun us. Shortly after the first Sony Reader arrived on the market, the company created the Sony Reader Library Program. Instructions for locating a participating library and checking out e-books are prominently displayed on their website. Libraries receive free e-readers and a variety of promotional materials. Because Sony uses the standard EPUB file format, the company promises purchasers of their e-readers that they can get e-books from a variety of vendors, but they make it especially easy to download from the online Sony Reader Store. The store is not only well supplied with recent books but links to Google's vast collection of public domain titles as well. At this writing, Sony has introduced a new tablet computer intended to compete with the Kindle Fire and Barnes & Noble's Nook Tablet. It is worrisome that at this writing, Sony is not accepting new libraries into the program, and we can't help but wonder whether things are going well. Another downside is that Sony's market share in the United States is not large. It seems to do better in Europe and Asia, but the United States is, of course, the largest market.

Other Competitors

As mentioned above, the Nook is Barnes & Noble's e-reader entry into the market. It comes with a feature that allows readers to lend their e-books to other Nook owners for two weeks and has quite a lot of space for users' own personal content. The Nook also uses the nonproprietary EPUB file format and so is compatible with library e-book collections. The newest Nook boasts "GlowLight" which illuminates the e-ink screen, allowing readers to enjoy the higher e-ink quality and still read comfortably under low light conditions.

The Kobo Company based in Toronto has introduced its own e-ink products to the market, the $80 Kobo Touch and the $180 Kobo Vox. Though their market share is not large, the company has many enthusiastic customers. The Spring Design Alex eReader is technically sophisticated but priced at $399, and is beyond the budgets of most people. However, its dual screens, one of which is a full-color touch screen and the other an e-ink screen, may attract high-end customers.

The iPad and Other Tablet Computers

Although e-readers have only been on the scene for a few years, their supremacy is being challenged by the emergence of small, easy-to-use tablet computers. Most people prefer e-ink-based readers to backlit computer monitors, but they perform one function and one function only. Ideally, most customers would like to be able to enjoy their e-ink screens on a small portable device that also acts as a fully functional personal computer. Netbook computers were the first to attempt to fill this need. They were much lighter in weight than traditional laptops and almost as convenient as dedicated e-readers. Nevertheless, it was somewhat burdensome to go through the usual computer procedures (e.g., startup, loading and unloading software) just to read a book. The arrival of Apple's iPad tablet revolutionized the market with a computer that was light in weight and which incorporated much of the convenience of dedicated e-readers. The iPad's 9" color display, instant page-turn, two-page layout, and computer functionality make it a very acceptable e-reader substitute for most users. It hasn't solved the problem of the backlit screen, but it can do so much more than a dedicated device that, at prices ranging from $499 to $630, it became an instant sensation and other companies rushed to get into the tablet market.

It was quickly discovered that the Windows operating system was not designed to work efficiently in the tablet environment and so most of Apple's competitors now use Google's Android operating system. Both Kindle and Barnes & Noble have come out with hybrids that are part e-reader, part Android tablet (at this writing, Sony has announced its own tablet with similar specs). Although they have backlit screens, both have found ways to make e-text look more like their dedicated, e-ink reader screens. Although most users still prefer reading e-ink, the new tablets are so small and so convenient that they are quickly making wide swaths across the marketplace. With a Nook Tablet or Kindle Fire tucked into purse or backpack, users need never be without access to their personal documents, e-mail, or the Internet. As cell phones become smarter and computers shrink, we are approaching a time when a large part of the population will have access to a computer wherever they are.

Reading Software

In addition to dedicated readers, most vendors like Amazon and Barnes & Noble also provide software that can be installed on smartphones, as well as Android, Apple, and Windows computers, allowing users to purchase, download, and read the books for sale on their websites. Though smartphones have very small screens, it may be hard to justify spending two or three hundred dollars on another device when you can download a book to your phone. Blio is free e-reader software that's not format-specific and can be loaded on almost any computer. Users thus have a lot of options when it comes to reading their e-books. It remains to be seen whether dedicated e-readers will continue to thrive or be replaced by multifunctional alternatives.

So how will all this impact the future of the book? The Pew Internet and American Life Project released its report on the "The Rise of E-Reading" in April 2012.[8] It found the following:

- One-fifth of adults have read an e-book in the past year.
- The average e-book reader has read 24 books in the past year. This number was much higher than for readers of printed books.
- 41 percent of tablet computer owners and 35 percent of owners of e-reading devices say they spend more time reading now than they did in the past.
- On a typical day, four times as many people are reading e-books than was the case two years ago.
- 42 percent of readers of e-books depend primarily on a computer, 41 percent of readers of e-books use dedicated e-readers like Kindles or Nooks, 29 percent of readers of e-books do so on their cell phones, and 23 percent of readers of e-books depend on a tablet computer.

- Survey respondents preferred e-books to print for speed, accessibility, and portability. They preferred printed books when reading to children or sharing books with others.
- More than half of e-book users prefer to buy rather than borrow.
- People who read e-books are more likely to be under age 50, have some college education, and live in households earning more than $50,000.

Although there are definitely advantages (like color illustrations) to printed books, it is obvious that the e-reader business is booming. Early assumptions that the public would not accept e-readers appear to be unfounded. E-book prices are often higher than paperback prices and may be much higher than used books. However, it seems inevitable that the number of printed books will decline, so fewer used books will be available. Libraries can't afford to hide their heads in the sand. If libraries are to flourish in the twenty-first century, e-book circulation will need to become a high priority.

NOTES

1. Alvin Toffler, *The Third Wave* (New York: Morrow, 1980).
2. Jeannette Woodward, "Auto Aces or Accident Victims: Librarians on the Information Superhighway," *American Libraries,* November 1995.
3. Jeannette Woodward, *Countdown to a New Library: Managing the Building Project* (Chicago: American Library Association, 2000).
4. Jeannette Woodward, *Countdown to a New Library: Managing the Building Project*, 2nd ed. (Chicago: American Library Association, 2010).
5. "Does the Brain Like E-Books?" *New York Times Online*, April 18, 2010, http://roomfordebate.blogs.nytimes.com/2009/10/14/does-the-brain-like-E-books/.
6. Ibid.
7. Ibid.
8. Pew Research Center, Pew Internet and American Life Project, "The Rise of E-Reading," April 5, 2012, http://libraries.pewinternet.org/files/legacy-pdf/The%20rise%20of%20e-reading%204.5.12.pdf.

RESOURCES

"Books Have Many Futures." *Library Administrator's Digest* 45, no. 8 (October 2010): 58–59.

Deahl, R. "How E-Book Sales Compare to Print . . . So Far." *Publishers Weekly* 257, no. 43 (November 1, 2010): 4.

Helgren, J. E. "Booking to the Future." *American Libraries* 42, no. 1/2 (January/February 2011): 40–43.

Milliot, J. "Digital Reader Penetration Accelerates." *Publishers Weekly* 257, no. 47 (November 29, 2010): 3.

Mueller-Hanson, R. A., et al. "Preparing to be 'Future Ready.'" *Information Outlook* 15, no. 4 (June 2011): 15–17.

Mulvihill, A. "iRise: Visualizing the Future." *Information Today* 28, no. 7 (July/August 2011): 28.

"Pulping the Hardback?" *Library Administrator's Digest* 46, no. 2 (February 2011): 14.

Robinson, C. W. "The March of the E-Books" [commentary]. *Library Administrator's Digest* 45, no. 8 (October 2010): 6.

LIBRARIES VS. E-PUBLISHERS

THE LIBRARY'S POINT OF VIEW

Central to an analysis of the library's future is an understanding of the role of digital materials, especially the dramatic success of e-books in the marketplace. Librarians, of course, have not been sitting idle, and most libraries lend e-books on a routine basis. However, the relationship between libraries and e-book publishers is in its infancy and has not thus far been very cordial. E-books have not really taken off in most libraries, and librarians tend to blame both publishers and distributers like Amazon for putting unnecessary barriers between library users and e-books. Publishers, for their part, are very wary after the near deathblow dealt to the music industry by illegal downloading. Many are not anxious to work with libraries.

WORKING WITH E-BOOK PUBLISHERS

Libraries have been anxious to increase e-book circulation because the electronic format is popular and engages some readers who may view printed books as antiques. However, they have discovered the titles they need are often unavailable. E-book distributors sometimes fill their catalogs with less popular titles while best sellers are unavailable. A high school teacher in New York made a determined search for e-texts to support English classes. One would imagine that since these tended to be older books, they would not be hard to find. However, she was able to obtain fewer than half the needed titles. When informally sampling titles supplied by some e-book services, librarians have found large numbers of books in the public domain that are freely available through the Google Books program.

Why are so few front-list titles available through the distributors serving libraries? In general, the answer is that publishers won't work with them. Penguin opted out of a distribution agreement with OverDrive, which provides content distribution to many libraries in the United States. Penguin will no longer sell its e-books and audiobooks directly to libraries or make them available through services that supply libraries. At this writing, Penguin is said to be negotiating continuance agreements with libraries to allow distribution of works that have already been purchased, but it is not open to a future relationship. The publisher made its decision after Amazon decided to allow libraries to lend Kindle content.

HarperCollins has notified the vendors that provide e-book services to libraries that their books may be circulated only twenty-six times before the license expires. HarperCollins has also requested personal information about the people who check out e-books, information that librarians have scrupulously guarded. Random House has expressed its commitment to continue working with libraries, but in March 2012 the publisher tripled the price it charged library e-book distributors. The price of a book that sold for about $20 in print rose to about $120 when obtained through OverDrive. However, all its front-list and backlist titles are available for library lending. Macmillan does not make e-books available to libraries with the exception of Palgrave Macmillan, a subsidiary that publishes scholarly titles. Simon & Schuster e-books are not available for library lending, but digital audio titles are.

In Britain, the Publishers' Association announced a policy for library lending of e-books that certainly does not meet the libraries' needs, but it at least opens the door to further communication. Stephen Page, CEO of Faber and Faber, addressing a library conference in the United Kingdom, said that if libraries start lending e-books, it could serve to "undo the entire market for e-book sales."[1] The policy propounded by the Publishers' Association would require that library users come to the library's physical premises to download e-books at library computers onto their mobile devices. There would be no remote downloading. The fee paid by the library would cover the right to lend one copy to one individual at any given time, and users would be strictly limited by the library's geographical service area. Page went on to say, "We will now work with the digital library suppliers to ensure that this service can be quickly brought to libraries."[2] Much of the attraction of e-books is their convenience. Bringing one's mobile device to the library and then connecting it to the library's computer system seems fraught with problems. The procedure could endanger the security of both the customers' devices and the library's computers. The policy even seems to preclude the possibility of a wireless download within the library. Circulating e-books thus becomes considerably less convenient than circulating printed books for both the library staff and their customers.

Sources of Conflict

Library e-book procedures have been evolving over the last few years and follow essentially the same pattern as printed books. E-books are checked out for the library's standard loan period, become inaccessible after that time unless renewed, and may not be used by more than one library user at a time. In other words, it would seem that neither libraries nor library users can exploit publishers of e-books any more than they can exploit publishers of printed books. While some best sellers may eventually circulate many times, other less popular books are checked out much less often and are made available by libraries as a public service (or perhaps as the result of a poor selection decision). Many of us think the average number of times a library book circulates is nowhere near as large as publishers imagine and has far less impact on sales. The right of libraries to purchase single copies of books for the use of multiple patrons has long been established, but whether from fear or greed, publishers are hoping to rewrite the playbook. In their efforts to stabilize their own industry, they sometimes appear to be taking direct aim at libraries.

Licensed, Not Owned
Although one must sympathize with publishers who have watched the music business go down in flames because of illegal downloading, their response may be so extreme as to threaten one of the most basic library functions. When libraries purchase a printed book, they own it. They are, of course, limited by the copyright law but with the exception of unlawful use, they can pretty much do what they like with the book. On the other hand, libraries merely purchase a license to use an e-book in accordance with a set of strict conditions laid down by the publisher and the service provider. These rules are enforced by the software used to download and access the e-books, but they also have legal standing since they are part of the terms of use agreement. Vendors providing distribution services are subject to the restrictions imposed by the publishers and may impose additional restrictions to make sure they are not caught uncomfortably in the middle. Under these conditions, libraries have few options. If a library refuses to accept the conditions imposed on it, its customers no longer have access to these titles.

The Amazon Experience
Libraries, of course, are not the only customers affected by licensing agreements. You may remember a few years ago when Amazon remotely deleted some digital editions of George Orwell's *1984* and *Animal Farm* from all Kindles. Apparently, these books were added to the Kindle store by a company that did not have rights to them, and Amazon was asked to remove the illegal copies from customers' devices. It shocked Kindle owners to realize that the e-readers and electronic files they had purchased were completely controlled and monitored by Amazon. Amazon had it in its power to add, remove, or change any Kindle content. Even the personal notes that students and other readers made for their own use were erased.

The implication was not lost that *1984* concerns a totalitarian "big brother" society where government censorship consisted of erasing all traces of news articles embarrassing to Big Brother by sending them down an incineration chute called the memory hole. As Charles Slater, a Philadelphia sheet-music retailer, complained, "Of all the books to recall, I never imagined that Amazon actually had the right, the authority or even the ability to delete something that I had already purchased."[3] British Telecom security expert Bruce Schneier agrees. "As a Kindle owner, I'm frustrated. I can't lend people books and I can't sell books that I've already read, and now it turns out that I can't even count on still having my books tomorrow."[4]

Demise of the First Sale Doctrine

Although Amazon's action was unwise from a marketing perspective, it was probably legal. The issues are complex. E-books are still in their infancy and many judicial decisions will be needed before conflicting interpretations are all resolved. However, the *Vernor v. Autodesk* decision handed down on September 10, 2010, by a federal appeals court struck a major blow to what's known as the "first sale doctrine," an interpretation which had been in place for more than a hundred years. In essence, the old legal interpretation held that when you buy a book or other item, it's yours. You have the right to lend it or resell it. However, the recent court decision views e-books as totally different from printed books. They are computer files and, therefore, are considered to be in the same category as computer software. Customers purchase only a license to use them; they do not own them.

Because the decision could potentially threaten the future of library lending practices, the American Library Association, the Association for College and Research Libraries, and the Association of Research Libraries joined a coalition in support of the first sale doctrine. Together with the Electronic Frontier Foundation, the Consumer Federation of America, the U.S. Public Interest Research Group, and Public Knowledge, they filed an amicus curiae brief with the U.S. Court of Appeals for the Ninth Circuit in support of plaintiff Timothy Vernor, an online software reseller. They argued that the first sale doctrine promotes access to knowledge, preservation of culture, and resistance to censorship. The library community understands that businesses and individuals must be compensated for their labor, and the ability to legally make unlimited copies of an e-book, music file, or software program would remove the incentive to create, innovate, and conduct business. However, allowing digital publishers to make all the rules and impose any restrictions they choose is an equally unsatisfactory solution.

Kindles and OverDrive

Initially, Amazon's terms of use agreement made it clear that the company was not willing to work with libraries, and a practice such as the one described above would probably be considered illegal. Then in April 2011, Amazon announced a partnership with OverDrive that would allow library users to borrow Kindle books. Library lending was made available for all generations of Kindle readers and free Kindle reading apps. Libraries subscribing to the service automatically see these Kindle editions in their OverDrive catalog. Because the Kindle OverDrive Agreement breaks so much new ground, I'll briefly summarize the instructions that Amazon provides to users.

After explaining how to identify libraries that subscribe to the OverDrive service, library users find the desired title from the OverDrive catalog and begin the library checkout process. They follow the library's normal procedure, using their library card ID and PIN to complete the checkout. Then they click on "Get for Kindle" and are redirected to the Amazon site. Here they must log in to Amazon. If they don't already have an account, they must create one, sharing whatever personal information Amazon requires. Finally, they choose their device and click on "Get Library Book" to have the file sent to them via the library's wireless connection. Some titles may not be delivered to the customer's personal reading device. Instead, they must be transferred from a library computer to the customer's device by USB cable.

Obviously, the ability to borrow Kindle e-books from the library is an attractive service, but it seems as if both Amazon and the publishers are determined to make it as unattractive as possible. Take, for example, the requirement that the library user create an Amazon account. The company maintains quite a bit of information about its Kindle customers, the kind of information that libraries do not make available to vendors or even government agencies without a search warrant. Then consider the requirement that some titles must first be downloaded to a computer and then transferred to the reading device using a USB cable. Making such a transfer requires considerable technical skill. Much of the appeal of Kindles and other e-readers lies in the fact that they are so user-friendly and require so little technical skill. Most librarians would agree that a fairly large percentage of their customers could not perform this procedure without a lot of handholding by library staff members.

ReadersFirst Initiative

Largely in response to demands like these, a group of libraries has banded together to pressure publishers and distributors to deal fairly with libraries. Currently at 109 library systems, the group plans to take advantage of its combined buying power to effect change. They are asking e-content providers to offer products that allow users to do the following:

- Search and browse a single comprehensive catalog with all of a library's offerings at once, including all e-books, physical collections, programs, blogs, and donor opportunities. Currently, content providers often only allow searches within the products they sell, depriving users of the comprehensive library experience.

- Place holds, check out items, view availability, manage fines, and receive communications within individual library catalogs or in the venue the library believes will serve them best, without having to visit separate websites (libraries, not distributors, should be enabled to manage all interactions with users).
- Seamlessly enjoy a variety of e-content. To do this, libraries must be able to choose content, devices, and apps from any provider or from multiple providers, without bundling that limits a library's ability to serve content it purchases on platforms of its choice.
- Download e-books that are compatible with all readers, from the Kindle to the Nook to the iPad and so on.

Old Friends to the Rescue?

In this challenging environment, one of the most promising developments is the entrance of some old library friends into the e-book marketplace. For example, the 3M Company has been working with libraries for more than forty years, developing the Tattle-Tape system, 3M SelfCheck, bar codes and RFID tagging, and many other innovative solutions that have been profitable for 3M and meet important library needs. 3M is a powerhouse of a company with extensive resources but, even better, 3M knows and understands libraries. The company has recently introduced the Cloud Library e-book lending service, which stands a very good chance of becoming one of its popular library solutions. At this writing the program has advanced from beta testing to installations in a large number of "early adopter" libraries.

The 3M Cloud will allow users to borrow digital books using their own iPads, Nooks, Android-based tablets, and most other devices. While policies are still somewhat in flux, there are definitely indications that 3M sees the e-book environment from the library's point of view. At this point, 3M platform fees are somewhat lower than competitors' and e-books seem reasonably priced, considering publishers' pricing policies. Although 3M must honor publisher restrictions, they don't seem to be imposing more hurdles of their own. For example, library users can download e-books from home directly to most devices. The cloud environment simplifies the process, although librarians tell me there are still some kinks to be worked out. Generic e-readers are available for checkout if customers don't have their own devices. Since the program is in its infancy, there are still too many ifs and buts, but the company seems committed to creating the best system possible, considering the constraints under which it must operate.

Another old library friend is Baker & Taylor. The company's entry in the e-book stakes is the Axis 360 Library Service with its Blio e-book reader software. The free software is designed to read e-books on almost any tablet computer, cell phone, android device, or netbook. Blio actually lays out pages like a printed book, with typography and illustrations included. The software includes many of the more sophisticated features of e-readers like Kindle and Nook, including note-taking capability and integrated web browser. At this point, the program isn't quite ready for prime time, but things look promising. For example, the service is tightly integrated with the library's circulation module and ordering is streamlined through the integration of print and electronic catalogs. The company currently has about 230,000 titles available and has signed a distribution agreement with Smashwords for an additional 100,000 independently published e-books representing 37,000 small presses. The big question, however, is how much progress has Baker & Taylor made with the big six, the heavy-hitting publishers who have thus far been less than cooperative?

As a profession, we have always enjoyed working with smaller companies that provide individualized services to libraries. However, many of us are increasingly getting the feeling that libraries are being outgunned in the e-book arena and it's time to send in the heavy artillery. In years past, publishing houses were human-sized entities. Now the big six control the industry and they, in turn, are units of vast, international corporations. 3M and Baker & Taylor are the best we can do in the way of big guns. We're all keeping our fingers crossed that they have what it takes to win the battle. If that isn't possible (and things are certainly looking bad), we hope that they will be able to negotiate a peace treaty that we can all live with until the dust settles and both libraries and publishers get some experience with digital resources.

THE SHRINKING IMPORTANCE OF THE LIBRARY MARKET

It is not difficult to understand why publishers don't want their customers choosing to download free e-books from their home computers rather than pay the full cost of their books. Publishers are naturally feeling threatened by the transition from printed books to e-books and may feel they need to shore up their sales in any way they can. In the past, publishers made their peace with libraries because a significant amount of their business came from libraries. Of course, they would have preferred that all those library customers buy, rather than borrow, their books, but turning their backs on the library market was not good business. At this point, libraries do not represent a large market for e-books and, frankly, publishers are scared of us. They have watched as music stores like Tower and Virgin closed their doors and large record labels were forced into bankruptcy because of illegal downloading.

Some libraries have gotten around restrictions by simply purchasing e-readers, loading them with customer-requested e-books, and circulating the two together. In other libraries, customers choose their e-books and staff download files to library e-readers as part of the checkout process. Public libraries are often burdened with extra copies of best sellers no longer needed after their fifteen minutes of fame expire. If loaded on e-readers, these files can be simply deleted and "hotter" titles substituted. These were necessarily small, do-it-yourself, experimental programs but they probably frightened some e-publishers. When e-readers were new to the market, they were expensive, so lending large numbers of e-readers stuffed with popular titles would have been cost-prohibitive. Now that a Kindle can be purchased for under $80 and other e-readers are similarly priced, libraries might easily decide that this is a cost-effective way to keep up with demand. Publishers, however, view such strategies as further reducing their sales.

E-Book Distribution
Libraries respond that if publishers would simply make their e-books available through a service like OverDrive, there would be no temptation to circulate large numbers of e-readers or find other ways to get around restrictions. The service would make certain that publishers' wishes were respected. However, I'm quite sure publishers would insist that that does not solve the problem. Stop for a moment and think about a customer who logs onto the library website, clicks on a service like OverDrive, and downloads a title. It may require a few extra clicks, but the experience is nearly identical to purchasing an e-book from a distributor like Amazon. The book descriptions are similar, the graphics are similar, and the time required to download the book is similar. What is not similar is that the library e-book is free. Why, publishers reason, should anyone choose to purchase the book?

The librarian responds that this has always been the way. Before the arrival of e-books, customers might choose to visit the bookstore or the library. Some readers chose to purchase and own their books, others chose to borrow them. Unfortunately, that response is a little self-serving. Of course, that isn't all there is to it. The library customer borrows a used book, a volume that has been handled by any number of other people. It may have a damaged cover, a missing page, a peanut butter glob on page 12, and yellow highlighted sections that must have seemed especially pithy to some past reader. If library customers were seeking best sellers, they had to get on a waiting list and make another trip to the library when the book became available.

On the other hand, customers who purchased books got something very different. They received a pristine, nearly germ-free volume that was much more attractive than the library's copy, could be used for personal note taking, and could be resold or kept permanently on their own bookshelves. Best sellers were immediately available, requiring no return trip to the bookstore.

When customers download library e-books, what do they get? They get files. When Amazon customers download e-books, what do they get? The answer is obvious; they get files. Is Amazon's file any handsomer than the library's? Are the library's e-books any germier, any more likely to have missing pages or other imperfection? Of course not! Perhaps even more important, e-book purchasers have little more control over their books than library customers. They cannot resell them or lend them to friends (unless the distributor makes special provision to do so). When you get right down to it, the license sold by the e-book vendor is little different from the e-book lent by the library except that the library's file becomes unusable at the end of the loan period. Yes, of course, it's nice to keep a book for as long as one likes, but is it a good enough reason to blow ten dollars on it?

The Demise of the Middlemen

Not only are e-book publishers wary of libraries, but it is difficult for libraries to find distributors that are willing to work with them and are sensitive to their needs. The distribution channels on which we have long depended for printed books are in a state of disarray. At this writing, Barnes & Noble is for sale, Borders is bankrupt, Canada's Fenn & Company is bankrupt, and Baker & Taylor has absorbed Blackwell of North America. Struggling for their very survival, these and other vendors have often failed to make a smooth transition to the digital environment. This means that libraries must deal with a limited number of service providers like OverDrive that are still interested in the library market. Often, these are relatively small companies that lack long-established relationships with major e-publishers. Even when publishers have not restricted library access, popular e-books may still not be available to library users. There has also been a tendency on the part of some publishers to dump books that have not been selling well into these services as a way to get a few more dollars out of soon-to-be remaindered titles. I remember going through one e-book distributor's catalog and being amazed that some of the books even existed; I couldn't imagine that anyone would want to read them.

GIVING OUR PATRONS WHAT THEY WANT

Yet sales of e-books are skyrocketing. Amazon has announced that it sells more e-books than paperbacks and hardbacks combined. When one considers how quickly the public has embraced the Kindle and other e-readers, the complacent comments of librarians about the feel and smell of real books seem rather foolish. Considering that even after recent price reductions, dedicated e-readers are still rather expensive, we must accept the fact that the reading public wants their books delivered to them in electronic formats. Obviously, we must find ways to obtain the most wanted e-books for our libraries or we risk losing customers. This means we must find ways to reassure publishers that working with libraries will not hurt their business, and we will probably need to accept some very inconvenient restrictions. At the same time, we must also find ways to keep our customers from being inconvenienced by squabbles between libraries and publishers.

The Cost Factor

From the perspective of most customers, e-books are expensive. They usually cost somewhat more than a mass-market paperback (about $10 for a typical novel) and roughly less than half as much as their hardback equivalents. Considering that they cannot be sold or traded for other titles, customers may see e-books as expensive. To publishers, however, e-books are painfully cheap because most publishing costs have little to do with ink and paper. Rather, it is editorial and marketing functions that account for most of the wholesale price of a book. Before the arrival of e-books, publishers first issued hardback editions, priced high to recoup most of these expenses. After a period of time, hardback sales dwindled and most publishers then issued paperback editions. Paperbacks are priced to cover production costs plus a little extra to make sure the publisher comes out in the black. If e-books competed only with paperbacks, publishers would have no cause for alarm. However, that does not seem to be the way things are going. E-books are increasingly eating into the hardback market, reducing the publishers' profit margins.

Nevertheless, the reading public is interested mainly in their own personal finances, and it certainly seems that many library customers would prefer to get their e-titles from the library. Lending e-books could well become the library's most popular service. It is not hard to see why publishers are worried about libraries. Yet libraries have reason to worry as well. Would customers refuse to borrow printed books? If the e-book version of a title were not available, would they borrow the library's hardback rather than purchase their own e-book? That's a question that's hard to answer. There's no doubt that the public is getting "hooked" on the convenience of e-books. In other words, e-books are habit-forming in just the same way that the habits of earlier generations drew readers to printed books. It is possible that at some point, customers will forgo printed books entirely and confine their library use to the titles we have available in electronic formats.

Amazon vs. the Publishers

One of the most important battles recently fought in the courts was the lawsuit filed by the Justice Department against the Apple Computer Company and several publishers, charging them with price fixing. To understand why the suit is so important, one needs to understand that there are two e-book pricing models competing to dominate the industry. The agency model allows publishers to freely set e-book prices and sell them directly to consumers through an "agent." The agent doesn't actually purchase the e-books but receives a percentage for facilitating the sale. What has come to be called the Amazon model gives retailers (like Amazon) the right to purchase e-books from publishers and price them any way they choose. Retailers are free to price e-books below-cost if that happens to be part of their marketing strategy. Publishers have naturally opposed the Amazon model because they fear that steeply discounted prices will ultimately make all e-book prices plunge, negatively impacting their profits. Apple took the side of the publishers to protect its own e-book sales against the giant Amazon, which controls such a huge share of the market. Publishers Simon & Schuster, Hachette Book Group, and HarperCollins settled out of court, but five other publishers are still charged with price fixing.

Too Few Publishers, Too Few Well-Fed Authors

Why is the case important to libraries? I think that in the midst of our own frustrations, we fail to remember that the publishing industry is in big trouble. At present, there are only six major commercial publishers. One by one, most of the presses that existed twenty or thirty years ago have gone. They were not profitable to run as independent enterprises and have either ceased to exist or been purchased by one of the big six. Librarians looking at the stack of catalogs that appear daily on their desks may think that there are lots of independent publishers. However, many of these are niche presses that publish a dozen titles a year or less and are operated as labors of love. This means that the work of their authors also becomes a labor of love as well. Very few writers make enough money to "quit their day jobs" and make writing their profession. While some books can be written in a few weeks, higher-quality works like biographies, histories, investigative reports, and literary works may require years of effort. Although libraries certainly purchase two-week wonders, they are committed to filling the information needs of their customers by making authoritative, well-written books more widely available. An important book published in 2011 that topped best-seller charts was Walter Isaacson's biography of Steve Jobs.[6] The 656-page book took many years to write, involved extensive travel and research, and required more than forty interviews with Jobs. Though it became a huge success, it failed to pay its author for the time and money he invested in its creation. One reason may be that Amazon is currently selling the Isaacson hardback (656 pages, remember) for $16.85. The Kindle edition goes for $14.99. Perhaps the book will become a Hollywood blockbuster, but Isaacson's experience has made it painfully clear to authors everywhere that they can't expect to earn a living from their craft.

How Long Will E-Books Be Around?

At this point, we can't be sure what the life expectancy of an e-book will be. Most of us have, in our personal libraries, books that are fifty or more years old.

Imagine how many file formats will come and go and how many gadgets will be marketed and discarded during the next fifty years. Vendors like Barnes & Noble and Amazon allow e-book files to be synced between electronic devices, but they certainly don't guarantee future access. At some point, it is certainly probable that your e-book will not be readable when you move on to a different type of device. In fact, the survival of e-book files will depend upon the survival of Amazon and other e-book vendors. Think of the number of publishing houses that have bitten the dust in the past fifty years. You might imagine what it would be like if the books that are now sitting on your bookshelves went up in smoke when the publishing house closed its doors or the bookstore from which you purchased them declared bankruptcy. Though not as dramatic a spectacle, that could be essentially what will happen to many e-books. As a reader, I think I might want to purchase the books I really value in print and turn to the library's e-book collection for the many leisure titles I have no desire to reread or add to my own personal collection. That may become the preferred option for tomorrow's readers.

Will Libraries Face Competition?

Even though libraries are not finding it easy to lend e-books, some private-sector businesses may still think there's money to be made in this area. Think about the example set by Netflix. In essence, Netflix circulates movies and television shows much like a library but the company charges customers a monthly fee. Suppose that large media retailers decide to build an e-book business based on the Netflix model. Customers would pay a flat monthly fee to download titles chosen from the company's catalog. However, the Netflix model involves sending out DVDs or streaming programs to subscribers. There is no danger of illegal downloads, so the service does not threaten media producers. Streaming is probably not an option with books, but files can be made unusable after a few weeks. Another business opportunity might resemble the cell phone service provider that offers customers a free phone if they sign up for a long-term contract. Imagine an e-book lending business that offers customers free e-readers if they pay a monthly fee and perhaps agree to a one- or two-year contract. If the company were large enough to negotiate with industry giants, e-book lending might prove to be a profitable business.

THE GOOGLE SUIT

Librarians occasionally speculate about different scenarios that might threaten their future well-being, and we must admit that some sound slightly paranoid. Google, of course, excites the paranoid tendencies of many businesses and institutions besides libraries. Google announced that it planned to get into the e-publishing business in 2011, and since it has already scanned a large portion of the world's printed books, the company is in an ideal position to make big money in the e-book market. Would Google be interested in lending the e-books in its vast library? It is certainly positioned to do so, but there's a lot more money in selling them.

Making predictions about the impact of digital resources on libraries is obviously fraught with pitfalls. Digital media have been available for such a short time that almost anything is possible. For libraries to be safe, secure, and successful in the future, they are going to have to live with e-commerce and e-commerce is going to have to learn to live with libraries. To illustrate this point, it might be useful to continue using Google as an example and take another look at its book project. In 2004 Google reached an agreement with several leading libraries, including Harvard and Stanford universities, the University of Michigan, Oxford University, and the New York Public Library. The libraries allowed Google to scan millions of their books, including many that were still under copyright. Google's stated goal was a noble one. The company would make the knowledge contained in the great libraries of the world available to millions of people. Noble though this goal might be, the thought of Google having such a huge resource under its control aroused the fears of libraries, publishers, and booksellers alike. A number of organizations, including the Association of American Publishers, sued Google for violating the copyright law.

In October 2009 an agreement was reached. Google agreed to pay $125 million and put its entire digitized library in "preview" format. Public libraries in the United States would be able to offer single terminals where full-text versions of the works would be available for free. If libraries chose to subscribe to a Google service, they would be given greater access to full text than the single terminal. The agreement, however, was not hailed by everyone and ultimately it was not accepted by the federal judge overseeing the case. On March 22, 2011, District Judge Denny Chin ruled in the case of *Authors Guild v. Google* that the settlement went too far and would have granted Google a "de facto monopoly." The settlement, Judge Chin wrote, would give Google too great an advantage over competitors. Google would be rewarded for copying copyrighted works without permission. The settlement released Google from liability for past wrongs and from future liability as well. Google would be empowered to sell access to copyrighted works and unclaimed works (often referred to as orphan works) that it had no legal right to.

Although the creation of a universal digital library would be of great value, the agreement was not fair. Although Amazon, Microsoft, copyright experts, and the Justice Department opposed the settlement, Judge Chin left the door open to a future agreement, saying that it might be possible to revise the agreement so that it might pass muster. As we know, copyright protection continues for seventy years beyond an author's death, protecting his or her heirs. The settlement would have allowed Google to presume it had the consent of unknown copyright owners unless owners made themselves known. The problem is, of course, that Google then would have access to works that others might like to republish. Most old books have little monetary value, but publishers would certainly be discouraged from publishing new editions if the title were easily available through Google.

Library Ideals vs. Library Realities

In the wake of the decision, librarians are divided on what it will mean to their profession. Some wonder whether Google could end up with a monopoly on human knowledge. Google has not had a sterling track record when it comes to using and misusing the private information of the computer users who depend upon its search engine. Google could potentially track the reading habits of its users just as e-commerce companies track the purchasing preferences of their own customers. Jonathan Band is the legal counsel for the Library Copyright Alliance, a group that represents the libraries that are members of three major copyright-related associations. In a panel at the National Press Club, he spoke on the implications of the Google agreement, concluding that libraries would be virtually forced to purchase institutional subscriptions to Google Book Search. "Faculty will insist upon it . . . students will insist upon it. There's a product they have to have, and in essence there's one supplier."[7]

On the other hand, many of us, especially academic librarians, were excited about the opportunity for improved access to information that the settlement offered, imagining low-cost subscriptions to the vast Google catalog. It is true that the HathiTrust Digital Library is available with its 5,516,126 book titles, 271,882 serial titles, and 3,639,746,950 pages. The HathiTrust is a partnership of major research institutions and libraries (more than sixty partners) for the purpose of contributing to the common good. It seeks to collect, organize, preserve, communicate, and share the record of human knowledge. At present, its resources are freely available on the Internet. However, large as the Hathi collection may be, the Digital Library has limited funding and Google offers the possibility of almost unlimited resources.

Despite the court decision, mass digitization projects have made much of human knowledge potentially available to the world. Although the focus has been on English-language publications, the floodgates have been opened and it is only a matter of time before various organizations scan most of the world's print output that has not been completely lost. Libraries certainly want to support the rights of copyright owners, but they know that many books simply disappear. Libraries have done much to preserve at least a copy of record for many publications, but it is not unusual for a work to be totally unavailable to scholars. If the rights of authors and publishers can be protected, a reworked agreement could allow Google to partner with libraries to preserve a huge portion of the world's knowledge.

Libraries and Other Digital Media

Of course, books are not the only type of media held by libraries. Music CDs, audiobooks, and DVDs account for much of the public library's circulation, and even academic libraries circulate a considerable quantity of non-print items. As the Internet got faster and able to send ever larger files, it became possible to stream short video clips via the Web and then full-length video programs. YouTube, begun in 2005, was the first widely used site for distributing thousands and later millions of short videos. As bandwidth has increased, YouTube became the source of millions of user-generated "viral" videos, classroom lectures, frolicsome kittens, and home video masterpieces. YouTube suffered a major setback when it was sued by Viacom for showing copyrighted content, but despite the loss of copyrighted material, YouTube has continued to be a top site because of the variety and sometimes bizarre nature of its content.

Netflix and Hulu

YouTube demonstrated that there was a big market for video content on the Internet, and commercial studios quickly realized that there was money to be made online. For a very modest fee, the Netflix service now provides nearly unlimited access to most television shows and commercial films. Customers can choose to have them mailed as postage-free DVDs or streamed over the Internet to their televisions or PCs. Watching movies on a computer monitor is not a very satisfying experience, and the technology can be daunting. Nevertheless, Netflix alone has over 23 million members, and most library customers can deal with these minor hurdles.

Fox, NBC, and their partners launched Hulu, a website that makes many full-length commercial television programs and movies available online, and other producers of video content soon joined them. Advertising content has made the site commercially successful, but so far, advertising has been less intrusive than the commercials that viewers must endure on cable and broadcast television. Hulu Plus is a premium service that provides additional content for a similarly modest monthly fee. Many cell phones and tablet computers come with the Hulu Plus app pre-installed so customers can watch their favorite shows anywhere anytime. The website includes social networking features, encouraging viewers to rate shows, comment on them, and argue with other viewers. This makes it possible to enjoy the content usually provided by television networks in the cozy social environment of the Internet.

Both of these services can be said to compete with library DVD circulation. However, by the time it began circulating non-print media, libraries had a long history of service and understood their responsibilities. For example, they understood that they were obligated to protect the privacy of their users. Not only library users' reading habits but also their viewing practices are highly personal and are nobody's business but their own. At present, Hulu is the defendant in a class action lawsuit charging that the company sells their customers' personal information to third parties without their consent. While libraries maintain very limited personal information about their patrons, Hulu keeps all the same basic data plus credit card numbers, program selections, and the text of endless arguments and discussions with other members. Similar lawsuits against other online content providers have been initiated, but this is new territory and the law is unclear.

There has always been a wide chasm separating the values of for-profit businesses and service organizations like libraries, but that chasm now resembles the Grand Canyon. Libraries provide popular films and television programs and they also proactively protect their customers against invasive and unethical practices. However, with Hulu offering free episodes of recent television shows and Netflix charging what amounts to pennies per film, it's hard to see how libraries can continue to compete. True, there are still many low-income patrons who can't afford either the membership fees or the technology needed, but libraries need a healthy mix of high-, low-, and middle-income patrons to be successful.

Libraries Organized around Physical Objects

The success of services like Hulu and Netflix, as well as the gradual merging of computer and television technologies, is impacting libraries in other ways as well. In a sense, this trend is totally different from the traditional library model built around different kinds of objects and different technologies (think audiocassette tape and audiocassette player, Betamax videocassette and Betamax videocassette player). Each type of object, as well as the device needed to use the object, is incompatible with other objects and devices, making it necessary to develop highly individualized policies and procedures. This means that libraries with their endless, perhaps dusty shelves can seem like dinosaurs to today's users, especially younger ones who cannot remember a time when they did not have a computer or a cell phone. Frustrated by the problems they encounter trying to provide digital media to their customers, libraries may feel the urge to stop time and continue to provide only materials that can be placed in boxes to which they can attach bar codes or RFID tags. However, if libraries are to survive and prosper, they must find a way to become digital media hubs.

Similarly, librarians are feeling hurt and angry at e-book publishers and distributors that appear to be making e-book lending as difficult as possible. We quite understandably believe that while we are nobly trying to serve the needs of so many people, vendors see us either as threats or as lucrative revenue streams. From my own personal perspective, I feel shocked at the speed with which e-books have overtaken print sales. There's a part of me that wants to cry out and declare that the public is wrong to abandon such beautiful and useful objects as printed books. However, we can't be ostriches hiding our heads in the sand. The phenomenal growth in e-book sales must alert us that this is the way of the future. We must find ways to provide the best and most popular titles to our customers in the formats of their choice. For example, if our customers buy Kindles, we must somehow find a way to provide Kindle e-book files. Our professional organizations must make peace with publishers and distributors without placing intolerable financial and procedural burdens on libraries. To be sustainable institutions in the twenty-first century, libraries must come to terms with the digital world and become full partners with the movers and shakers of that world.

NOTES

1. Benedicte Page, "PA Sets Out Restrictions on Library E-Book Lending," *ThE-bookseller.com.* October 21, 2010, www.the-bookseller.com/news/132038-pa-sets-out-restrictions-on-library-e-book-lending.html.

2. Ibid.

3. Brad Stone, "Amazon Erases Orwell Books From Kindle," *New York Times,* July 17, 2009, www.nytimes.com/2009/07/18/technology/companies/18amazon.html.

4. Ibid.

5. *ReadersFirst,* http://readersfirst.org.

6. Walter Isaacson, *Steve Jobs* (New York: Simon & Schuster, 2011).

7. Jack Stripling, "Life in a Google Book Search World," *Inside Higher Education,* August 12, 2009, www.insidehighered.com/news/2009/08/12/google.

RESOURCES

Aaltonen, M., et al., "Usability and Compatibility of E-book Readers in an Academic Environment: A Collaborative Study." *IFLA Journal* 37, no. 1 (March 2011): 16–27.

"Amazon, OverDrive to Launch Library Lending for Kindle." *Advanced Technology Libraries* 40, no. 6 (June 2011): 1, 11–12.

Breeding, M. "Preparing for the Long-Term Digital Future of Libraries." *Computers in Libraries* 31, no. 1 (January/February 2011): 24–26.

"E-book Lending Model Tested by Libraries and Publishers." *Library Journal* 136, no. 7 (April 15, 2011): 15.

Fialkoff, F. "It's Not About HarperCollins" [Editorial]. *Library Journal* 136, no. 6 (April 1, 2011): 8.

Goldberg, B. "Librarians Sing the E-book Blues." *American Libraries* 42, no. 3/4 (March/April 2011): 12.

Harris, C. "Rethinking HarperCollins." *School Library Journal* 56, no. 4 (April 2011): 15.

Mulvihill, A. "Librarians Face E-book Acquisition Obstacles." *Information Today* 28, no. 5 (May 2011): 13.

Ojala, M. "Challenging E-book Lending Policies." *Information Today* 28, no. 4 (April 2011): 1, 36–37.

Sellers, C. L., et al., "The Future of Library Collections." *Law Library Journal* 102, no. 4 (Fall 2010): 665–68.

Zimerman, M. "E-Readers in an Academic Library Setting." *Library Hi Tech* 29, no. 1 (2011): 91–108.

THE AGE OF
HIGH ANXIETY

THREATS THAT FUEL LIBRARY NIGHTMARES

Perhaps the only way to have a good shot at predicting the future is to correctly identify current trends that, to use a trite expression, have legs. In other words, we can all look around and see that a variety of things are happening to a number of libraries. Some of what we observe is strictly local. It may seem as if everyone is talking about it. Wherever you go, you keep hearing about it and perhaps you observe it in your own library. However, your professional world is small. You tend to talk with the same people again and again; you attend the same conferences and even hear the same presenters. If you read widely, you get a broader perspective, but authors have a bad habit of jumping on bandwagons. Even highly respected professional journals have sometimes failed to differentiate the "flash in the pan" from the transformative trend that will soon be rocking the library world. I'm afraid I'm probably one of those authors who has failed to see history being made. As I look at various disturbing trends, I wonder if I should be frightened and loudly sounding alarms. Do these trends represent dangerous threats or will they play a relatively small role in tomorrow's libraries?

THE THREAT OF OUTSOURCING

The first trend that worries many LIS professionals is outsourcing, the act of contracting out library services and functions to commercial businesses. Is this all a tempest in a teapot or will future libraries be operated for profit? If outsourcing should become the wave of the future, is this necessarily such a bad thing? To answer these questions, it is once again necessary to define our terms.

A number of library functions have been outsourced for years and for the most part, librarians feel little sense of alarm. For example, computerization made it possible for larger book vendors like Baker & Taylor to eliminate much of the work involved in materials selection. Libraries created profiles that described their collection needs in considerable detail and vendors provided books and media that corresponded to the subject matter, reading level, and other specifications in the profile. Many larger libraries now depend heavily on such profiles and staff make only limited selections of individual items. Other libraries have found that the profiles fail to identify a large proportion of needed materials. Many vendors can catalog and process these materials before shipping them.

Such services, of course, reduce dependence on in-house staff and so they clearly meet the definition of outsourcing. (Come to think of it, outsourcing has been around at least since the Library of Congress began supplying libraries with catalog cards.) However, most librarians have accepted such developments as the natural outgrowth of modern technology. Although they have reduced the need for some library specialists like catalogers, most of us agree that it would be foolish not to take advantage of cost-cutting opportunities if the end result meets or exceeds established quality standards.

Functions Commonly Outsourced

Over time, it became clear that other library activities could sometimes be outsourced at a lower cost than they could be performed in-house. Some of these candidates include:

- Bar coding or affixing RFID tags
- Bookkeeping, accounting, and payroll preparation
- Database development
- Data recovery
- Deacidification
- Disaster recovery
- Document delivery
- Microfilming
- Network management
- Printing
- Retrospective conversion
- Subscription management
- Temporary staffing
- Website design and hosting

Government Libraries

During the 1980s, the U.S. government began contracting out the entire operation of certain agency libraries. In 1983 privatization was being touted as a largely untapped opportunity to reduce government waste, and federal libraries were identified as appropriate targets for outsourcing or privatization. Soon, the Environmental Protection Agency, the departments of Energy, Labor, and Housing and Urban Development, and the National Oceanic and Atmospheric Administration all sought outsourcing agreements with commercial entities. Even though this was a much more drastic step, it still didn't set off a great many alarms. Government libraries were seen as different. They came under the general heading of "special libraries," many of which are operated by for-profit organizations. Jokes about federal government inefficiency and mismanagement are legion, so it was thought by some, even in our own profession, that outsourcing might actually result in more efficient, functional libraries. If a contractor failed to perform as promised, it could be let go and replaced by another contractor. When agency administrators compared this process to the enormously difficult task of firing underperforming civil service employees, there was little question that outsourcing library operations could save significant tax dollars.

Outsourcing and the Recession

So if library functions have been outsourced for years, why are we suddenly so worried? To answer that question, it might be helpful if I describe a hypothetical example. Let's say that River City is experiencing hard times. Because home prices have dropped precipitously as a result of the recession, much of the city's revenue has dried up and the City Council is looking for ways to cut costs. Along comes the Can-Do Library Outsourcing Corporation with a plan that's hard to resist. Can-Do promises to provide River City with the same library services it currently enjoys for perhaps 25 percent less than the city is currently spending (they can save even more if the city is willing to accept some drastic changes). Since this represents a considerable amount of money, River City agrees and Can-Do takes over the library. More specifically, Can-Do will take over the management of the library. Both the building and the collection remain the property of River City. The library board will probably continue to function much as it always has and will continue to report to the City Council.

Naturally, the company expects to make a nice profit out of the contract, so it is going to need to find ways to cut library expenses drastically. Since staffing accounts for the lion's share of the library budget, major changes are inevitable. The library staff is now working for a private company, not the city. Their job security has evaporated. Can-Do will bring in its own managers and is probably under little obligation to retain current staff members. Neither is Can-Do obligated to pay the same salaries or provide the same benefits. Of course, every outsourcing agreement is different and some include special provisions to protect library staff members, but the money has to come from somewhere.

Outsourcing and Library Staffing

Can-Do probably assured the City Council that it would achieve most of its cost savings through better management and the elimination of waste, but few libraries are so badly managed that a nip here and a tuck there can result in huge savings. Can-Do also claims that it can achieve cost savings by centralizing and automating routine procedures, but, of course, the River City Library has been outsourcing many of its routine functions for years. Since Can-Do must keep library patrons reasonably happy if its contract is to be renewed, materials budgets cannot be slashed. Since savings must come from somewhere, most library outsourcers take a dim view of professional library positions. While it is in their interest to retain local clerical and paraprofessional staff, Can-Do doesn't have a lot of use for degreed librarians. If this were a special library, Can-Do would evaluate the need for retaining specialized subject expertise, but this is a public library. They will probably find it more cost-effective to keep most of their professional positions at corporate headquarters and limit local decision-making. It is for this reason that librarians are increasingly looking on outsourcers as the evil empire.

The Story of LSSI

To do justice to the businesses that provide library management outsourcing services, it seems only fair to look more carefully at a successful company that has a number of satisfied customers and a reputation for generally delivering what it promises. Library Systems and Services LLC (LSSI) was founded in 1981 by Frank and Judy Pezzanite to provide specialized computer applications for libraries. Frank was the developer of the MINI MARC minicomputer cataloging system and the BIBPRO IV bibliographic products software package. Providing other computer services to libraries was a natural next step. This was about the time when the federal government decided that privatizing a variety of government services would result in considerable savings to taxpayers. Initially, LSSI provided specific contracted services like retrospective conversion and systems management, but it soon became clear that it could tap into a much larger market. LSSI presently provides management and other services for the following federal libraries:

- Department of Energy
- Department of Veterans Affairs
- Export-Import Bank of the United States
- Federal Trade Commission
- Geological Survey
- Library of Congress
- National Agricultural Library
- Overseas Private Investment Corporation
- Smithsonian Institution
- Social Security Administration

EXPANDING OUTSOURCING TO PUBLIC LIBRARIES

Although LSSI continues to provide cataloging and processing services as well as collection analysis, long-range planning, surveys and needs analyses, it found that managing libraries could provide an even more lucrative market. After its success at winning federal contracts, it went on to become the first company to offer complete outsourcing to public libraries. To quote from its website, "We take full responsibility for developing and implementing your library's programs, technology plans, collection development, staff development, long range planning and the overall day-to-day management of the library."[1] Although it's difficult to get hard numbers, LSSI does employ library professionals, but the number compares unfavorably with libraries that have not been privatized. As was the case with our imaginary River City Library, library employees usually work for the contractor, not the library or local government. The company has been reluctant to discuss staffing practices, but it has admitted to some library boards and government agencies that paying lower salaries and benefits, hiring fewer librarians, and choosing less-educated employees all contribute to lowering its costs. Instead of continuing pension benefits, LSSI generally allows employees to contribute to a 401(k) plan to which the company adds an unspecified match.

With its background in library automation, the company usually does a good job of handling routine library operations. However, LSSI is known to cut corners where it can and its core mission is inevitably different from the traditional mission of the public library. As mentioned earlier, hard data about LSSI libraries is difficult to come by. Private companies are not subject to the same transparency requirements as government agencies. Non-disparagement clauses in LSSI contracts may prevent employees from discussing the company and its practices. However, some patterns have become evident. The company usually begins by investing considerable time and professional expertise in identifying library weaknesses, solving problems, and generally making a library function more efficiently. As time goes by, however, the company seeks to recoup its investment and gradually squeezes more money out of the library budget to shore up its profit margin. Librarians have reported pressure to cut services and increase staff workload without additional compensation. Similarly, materials budgets tend to drop when LSSI takes over a library.

Outsourcing and the Library Job Market

But let's get back to River City and see how the Can-Do Library Outsourcing Corporation has been getting along. At this writing, the recession has not fully abated and library jobs are scarce. This means that Can-Do has the upper hand. Most library staff members will probably choose to endure a reduction in salary and benefits just to stay in their home communities. Since Can-Do probably plans to do some staff pruning anyway, the few who choose to leave will only accelerate the planned budget reductions. Can-Do does not intend to employ many librarians or other professional staff, and the poor economy will ensure that it has sufficient applicants for library manager positions. Because employment depends on the continuance of local government contracts, these are hardly plum positions, but there are presently plenty of unemployed librarians who are willing to accept Can-Do's conditions.

Nevertheless, we have every reason to believe that the current employment situation is temporary. Librarians are retiring at a rate that is higher than in most other professions. What will happen when employment returns to pre-recession levels? There appear to be at least two likely scenarios. In the gloomier of the two, outsourcers will triumph. Local governments will gradually become accustomed to outsourcing library operations, and professionals in local librar-ies will become rare birds indeed. However, there is another possibility that many librarians consider the more likely one. As the economy improves and jobs become more readily available, library staff members will demand higher salaries and better benefits. Library professionals will also be choosier when more attractive options become available to them. Bear in mind too that the outsourcer is paying not only the library's bills but its own as well. The healthy economy will also mean that corporate expenditures will rise. Corporate execu-tives typically earn much higher salaries than library staff members, whether professional or paraprofessional. Outsourcers will no longer be able to offer local governments the "great deals" they once did and it will become increasingly clear to local government officials that "you get what you pay for." Despite what outsourcers might advertise about responding to community needs, they can only achieve significant savings by standardizing services. Local residents, library board members, and government officials alike cannot fail to be aware that the library template developed in Oshkosh does not translate very well to River City no matter how many needs assessments the corporation may conduct.

Will Public Libraries Go the Way of Federal Libraries?

Since the outsourcing of management services is a relatively recent develop-ment, we don't yet have very much data with which to evaluate the success or failure of outsourced libraries. However, there is evidence that federal govern-ment agencies are generally more satisfied customers than local governments. As mentioned earlier, federal libraries have long been viewed as set apart from the activities in which their agencies engage. Privatization has generally been found to save money since large bureaucracies generate considerable waste. In addition, career civil servants are often seen as more expensive and occasionally less productive than independent contractors. Agency heads know little about libraries and may view their supervision as an unwanted burden. Because the library may be seen as unrelated and perhaps irrelevant to the agency's opera-tions, it is not uncommon for agency supervisors to dump unwanted staff mem-bers on the library. Such negative attitudes become self-fulfilling prophecies, and so the library becomes more and more dysfunctional, resulting in greater marginalization. When a company like LSSI takes on such a library, it brings in its own well-trained managers, fires nonproductive employees, reduces staffing costs, and creates efficient procedures and policies; the result, of course, is seen as positive. Many government agencies, however, have excellent libraries staffed and managed by civil service employees, and outsourcing has not worked well in some other government libraries. Thus, it appears that the two management strategies will continue to coexist for the foreseeable future.

The Public Library Board of Directors

Is this a likely outcome for public library outsourcing? Most public libraries come under the direction of a board composed of local residents appointed by county or municipal government. Board members usually serve on a volunteer basis. When library services are outsourced, the role of the library board usually remains unchanged. The board continues to make policy decisions and work with LSSI or other corporate appointees in much the same way they did with city or county employees. Unlike federal agency heads, board members have assumed their library responsibilities willingly. In a sense, this allows them to be considerably more objective than federal agency heads seeking to lighten their own load.

Then, too, board members usually wear multiple hats. As local residents they are library customers and know much better than a remote government administrator whether the library is serving community needs. Though board members must be fiscally responsible and aware of the library's bottom line, they spend a considerable part of their time responding to complaints and resolving conflicts. They are far more likely to concern themselves with budget details than thrice-removed administrators and will notice cuts in materials and programming budgets. If the contract is to be profitable, the vendor must find money somewhere in the budget. Typically, library staff members come to the board when they believe they have not been treated fairly. If the vendor takes much of its profit from staff salaries, the outcry cannot help but find its way to the board, which will probably be sympathetic to the staff's demands. After all, these are neighbors whom board members know and care about. Whether seeking leisure reading suggestions or getting help with their local history research, they are less likely to see staff members as budget line items than administrators in a large bureaucracy would.

Will Outsourcing Lose Its Advantage?

What all this means is that in the future, a contractor like LSSI will need to provide improved library services and acceptable staff salaries and benefits, as well as significant cost savings. When one considers that public library budgets are rarely generous and staff salaries are low, considering the education and experience that library staff usually possess, it's hard to see where big money can be found. For the most part, contractors that provide management out-sourcing services have been successful in signing up library systems only when the systems have been in crisis. For example, tax revenue has dropped precipi-tously and a union contract prevents the system from scaling back to cope with the emergency. In a few situations, the library system is somehow broken, and library management is unable to deal with problems or provide the services demanded by the community. Bringing in an outside contractor is seen as a way to clean house and get a fresh start. In other words, vendors may be able to take advantage of situations that are not typical. Since most libraries are successful in providing needed services to their communities at moderate cost and local gov-ernments have rarely experienced budget shortfalls of this magnitude, it may be that the outsourced public library is the product of extreme circumstances, an anomaly spawned by the recession or some other crisis situation.

Are we mixing apples with oranges when we cite the privatization of some federal government libraries as evidence that public libraries are in danger? It is too early to make any definitive pronouncements, but it does seem as if the factors that encourage the trend in federal libraries do not exist elsewhere. The cost savings that may be accomplished by sidestepping large unwieldy bureaucracies and which make library outsourcing attractive to independent contractors don't seem to have a counterpart on the local level. When one considers that such cost savings must be sufficient to support a corporate management structure and generate dividends for stockholders, it becomes even less likely.

STAFFLESS LIBRARIES

To some extent, the employment of librarians has always been directly related to the difficulty of finding things in a library. Printed reference works and library catalogs were hard to use. They required insider knowledge like knowing which part of the call number should be read as a decimal and which part as a whole number. Alphabetization, which computers have made so easy, was once gov-erned by complicated, counterintuitive rules devised by librarians and editors. Before keyword searching became possible with computers, highly trained librarians were needed to translate the customer's need into searchable terms that could be found in the library classification system's controlled vocabulary.

Impact of Automation

Much of the highly specialized knowledge that was once needed to maintain a library is no longer relevant. If such knowledge is still required, computers have made it possible to share the expertise. For example, utilities like OCLC allow hundreds or even thousands of libraries to share a single cataloging record. Ven-dors provide materials that arrive cataloged and processed, making it possible for smaller libraries to function effectively without a professional cataloger. Computer search engines like Google can locate information in a fraction of the time that reference librarians once required and they can provide far more of it than can be housed in any but the largest libraries. Of course, library collections provide more reliable information than most websites and reference librarians know how to filter out unwanted and unreliable information. Nevertheless, in most instances, users no longer require an intermediary to find what they are looking for.

Will LIS Professionals Disappear?

Is it possible that there will come a time when local governments and academic institutions will be unwilling to pay for the professional skills that librarians possess? Might they continue to fund libraries that either function without a library staff or with only a clerk or two to keep tabs on the materials and perhaps operate some kind of document delivery service? Might even those few staff members be replaced by security cameras, self-checkouts, and automated RFID processing of materials? Could the future library look a lot like Contra Nostra County's Library-a-go-go or Sweden's "Bokomaten"? The GoLibrary, as it is also called, is a machine that requires only a small space, a dedicated high-speed Internet connection, and RFID tags to turn a vending machine into a library. San Francisco Bay area commuters can find libraries-a-go-go at several locations, each stocked with approximately 400 paperbacks that can be checked out to library cardholders. Customers make their selections using the touch screen and their book is delivered by a robotic arm.

Other librarians wonder whether the King's County Library System's unstaffed 300-square-foot Library Express @ Redmond Ridge could be the wave of the future. The express is an unstaffed facility that allows customers to pick up their holds, access the library catalog, and select from a small browsing collection of paperbacks. A dedicated phone makes it possible to speak with a staff member at the nearby Redmond Regional Library. Entering the small building by scanning their library card or typing their card number, customers depend for their security on cameras located both inside and outside the building. The Houston Public Library is experimenting with a similar staffless facility called the HPL Express which differs from King's County in that though small and quite limited in terms of service, it is staffed. Houston plans to install similar facilities in existing buildings, shopping malls, and airports. Wake County's Express Library Fayetteville Street is located inside the Wake County Office Building. Other library systems around the country are experimenting with similar small-scale attempts to create a library presence without a full-function library.

New Library Models

In themselves, these small library kiosks, vending machines, and pint-size facilities in convenient, high-traffic locations don't appear to pose a threat to libraries. They simply extend certain limited library services to people who might not otherwise have access to them. Four hundred paperbacks does not a library make. If this is clearly understood by decision-makers, the public gains a resource and the library expands its services. If, however, decision-makers make the mistake of imagining that these facilities are actually libraries and that they can meet the information needs of area residents, then they might indeed be cause for anxiety.

The majority of these services are focused on the need of library users to kill time while enduring the daily commute. They do not address the needs of children, young adults, or retirees. One wonders about the impact of these "expresses" on the library budget and on services to other library users. Actually, to call any of these facilities staffless is inaccurate. Someone, of course, must maintain them: cleaning them, restocking the collection, rebooting the computer, and performing a variety of necessary tasks. They are also relatively expensive, requiring security equipment including cameras, card-based door entry systems, and highly sophisticated RFID systems.

Service to Library Constituencies

Not only are there usually no staff members available on-site to assist customers, but the small browsing collections are unlikely to satisfy even the leisure-reading needs of many customers. There are no public Internet-enabled computers, no Wi-Fi, and no comfortable spaces where customers can get away from their daily grind and catch up on the latest newspapers and magazines. Nevertheless, those commuters are the people who pay taxes and support local government, including libraries. It is certainly true that libraries have done little to court them, often setting library hours for the convenience of staff and making it all but impossible for working people to visit the library. If libraries are to enjoy a happy, successful future, they must reach out to this group, but the question is how. Because of the recession, we are currently experiencing unprecedented budget cuts, but library budgets are always tight. There is no reason to think that the future holds the promise of generous library budgets. Tough choices must be made, and expensive services that serve one group may unfairly discriminate against another. Groups like children and the elderly may be unable to make their voices heard when they are in competition with middle-class adults who want little from the library but occasional diversion.

Staffless Academic Libraries

In the academic world, the term *staffless library* has a somewhat different meaning. Students use the library building as a quiet place where they can relax, prepare for class, or study for a test. They depend heavily on the library's public computers and on subscription databases that may not be available outside the library. Reference services have been in decline in academic libraries for a number of years, and the intellectually demanding reference queries of the past have all but disappeared. It is not surprising then that university administrators may wonder why there are so many relatively high-paid librarians on the payroll. Is there really a need for sophisticated skills when most of the work involves restocking shelves, resetting computers, and maintaining order? Although the number varies from library to library, academic libraries typically employ a larger proportion of professional staff than do public or school libraries. Is there truly a greater need for their services?

At the beginning of this chapter, I mentioned that we often fail to recognize the trends that presage the future. In talking with academic librarians, I find that they are fully aware of individual changes that have taken place in their libraries like the growth in popularity of self-checkout machines, the decline in circulation of some types of materials, and the gradual disappearance of reference librarians. However, they often fail to put it all together. They are not really aware that because fewer students and faculty interact with the library staff, the staff may no longer be on decision-makers' radar. From the point of view of college and university administrators, the library may already be nearly staffless, so why is the personnel budget so high?

Perhaps it is neither outsourcing nor staffless libraries that pose the real danger to libraries, but librarians who don't really understand why decision-makers find them attractive as targets for budget cuts. Perhaps it is a matter of being so absorbed in day-to-day problems that we fail to see ourselves as others see us— or perhaps as they don't see us. In other words, what our profession does not need is Harry Potter's famous cloak of invisibility. In some respects, we may have fashioned our own cloak and it may be the source of the problem.

Branch Libraries

As the present recession continues, an ever-larger number of public library branches are closing. With the drastic cuts in library budgets that are taking place around the country and around the world, it's probably inevitable that local government officials and library administrators should view branch libraries as legitimate targets. Shutting down a branch results in relatively large budget savings and from an administrative point of view, it's easier to accomplish than most other cost-cutting options. Closing a branch may appear to have little impact on the rest of the library system. Imagine a typical system with a number of departments and services and buildings. Each unit is dependent on the others, each interacts with and supports others. Then imagine the system as a kind of tree with centralized services like administration, cataloging, processing, and acquisitions forming the trunk and branch libraries, as their name implies, sprouting from the trunk and reaching out into the community. At first glance, it would seem as if the best way to cut costs is to prune branches. The trunk is left unharmed and the library system can continue to go about its business. However, this analogy fails to recognize that at the end of those branches are the library's customers; branch libraries are focused on customer service. Most of those functions performed in the central library are intended to support customer service. A good branch library becomes an integral part of its home community. It is human-size, not institution-size. It is located within walking distance of the community's schools, homes, and businesses; it hosts community gatherings and club meetings, and it understands community needs.

Focusing on Customer Service

As I say, closing a branch library is usually easier for administrators than performing surgery on multiple library departments, functions, and services. Personnel decisions are somewhat easier because the jobs simply disappear when the branch closes its doors. Most items in the collection are available elsewhere in the system, and other library functions and services are not usually impacted by the closure. What may not be considered, however, is that the system is drawing strength and vitality from those branches just as the tree is drawing life in the form of carbon dioxide from its environment. There is no question that there are unsuccessful branches that are not contributing to the vitality of their systems and probably need to be closed. Perhaps the population has moved away, the neighborhood has become dangerous, or transportation issues keep customers away. If a branch is no longer attracting enough customers to justify its cost, then perhaps the closure is justified. However, to close a healthy branch will, in the end, harm the entire system.

In the present unhappy financial environment, budgets must certainly be pared down to the bone, but the overriding consideration should be minimizing the impact on the public. Dollar for dollar, branches probably have more interaction with and provide more direct service to the public than other library units. We sometimes imagine that if we cut public services, there will be a corresponding public outcry that will somehow result in budget increases. Although this strategy has occasionally worked, the opposite has more often been true. Customers are more likely to abandon the library because it no longer meets their needs.

When we speak of dangers to the library like outsourcing and staffless libraries, we are certainly dealing with very real issues that could negatively impact the library's future. However, I can't help but wonder if any such threat from the outside could be as dangerous as the poor decisions we ourselves sometimes make. No matter whether we are dealing with a public, academic, school, or special library, we have a responsibility to look beyond today's financial crisis and see the library as it evolves into its future identity. Our decisions must ensure that the library gets back on its figurative feet as quickly as possible and stands ready to play a vital role in the twenty-first century. If somehow we allow the library to go into hibernation, if it fails to evolve to meet tomorrow's needs or if the roles of LIS professionals fail to evolve, we will have done a grave disservice to our communities. Libraries can withstand all kinds of threats like the ones discussed here, but they cannot become irrelevant.

NOTE

1. "Library Management Services," *LSSI*, http://lssi.com/management.html.

RESOURCES

"Anger as a Private Company Takes Over Libraries." *Library Administrator's Digest* 46, no. 5 (May 2011): 33–34.

Choy, F. C. "From Library Stacks to Library-in-a-Pocket: Will Users Be Around?" [part of special issue "Academic Librarian: Singing in the Rain," part 2]. *Library Management* 32, no. 1/2 (2011): 62–72.

Czesak, C. "Having the Outsourcing Conversation." *Public Libraries* 50, no. 2 (March/April 2011): 17–18.

Hartmann, M. K. "Show Me the Money: Privatization and the Public Library." *Illinois Library Association Reporter* 29, no. 1 (February 2011): 4–7.

Kniffel, L. "Economy Is the Undoing of Libraries for the Future." *American Libraries* 40, no. 5 (May 2009): 19.

Matarazzo, J. M., et al. "Ignore the Idea of Outsourcing at Your Peril." *Public Libraries* 50, no. 2 (March/April 2011): 19–20.

Page, D. "The Threat of Privatization." *Arkansas Libraries* 68, no. 1 (Spring 2011): 8–9.

Robinson, C. W. "LSSI." *Library Administrator's Digest* 46, no. 5 (May 2011): 38–39.

4 THE LIBRARY IN CYBERSPACE

W ith very few exceptions, libraries of all types have acquired some kind of online presence. However, I think it is safe to say that, also with few exceptions, libraries don't fully participate in the societal transformation that is the Internet. On the one hand, libraries embraced computers more rapidly than most organizations, moving to networked cataloging and integrated systems in the early years of automation. Computers seemed to be designed just for the kind of record-keeping that occupied so much library staff time. Early catalogs were loaded with glitches, but the ability to search both by subject and keyword was revolutionary. Records that filed themselves also warmed the hearts of library staff members unless their jobs were made redundant. Thus we thought of ourselves as being in a high-tech profession, and because we could interact with library software and communicate by e-mail, we thought of ourselves as tech-savvy. The professionals who developed digital libraries soared ahead and some of these colleagues are still on the cutting edge of information studies.

DID LIBRARIES FALL BEHIND?

Though early on we claimed technology as our own turf and our public computers drew large numbers of users to the library, it seems that we have not been so successful with recent trends. It's hard to say precisely when we began losing ground, but it may be that we failed to equate technology with communication. For example, we used e-mail primarily to communicate with our colleagues and treated those messages like the memos that sat in our in-baskets for days until we found time to respond. I apologize to the authors of a certain journal article yet again for taking their names in vain. In fact, this time I will not even mention their names or the title of the infamous article. They innocently provided my "Aha!" moment when I suddenly realized one important reason why we were going astray. The article described a project that seemed quite daring. Students could text the reference desk of their university library. Since text messaging was quite new at the time, it sounded like a cool, trendy service. However, as I read further, I discovered that the phone number to which messages were sent was that of a company located a thousand or so miles from the library. The library had contracted with them to convert text messages into e-mail and redirect them to the library's reference desk. In publicizing the service, the library promised that students would receive a response within three business days. In other words, library users might receive a response about as quickly if they'd typed a memo on a sheet of paper, addressed it to the library, and sent it through campus mail. Librarians were still viewing electronic communication like the paper-based correspondence of fifty years ago.

For most people, the Internet means instant communication with another individual or group of "friends." Anyone sending a text message to the library would naturally expect a reply within minutes if she knows the library is open and staff are on duty. That's the nature of the medium. My quick Google search brought up a variety of sometimes conflicting statistics, but the average mobile phone owner sends about 400 text messages a month. The average teen sends about eighty texts a day. Add to that number the billions of Twitter tweets and instant messages and you begin to have a sense of the potential disconnect between the library and its users.

The Transition to Digital Resources

I've described in chapter 8 the experience of passing a classroom where a library literacy class was in progress. The librarian/instructor was in the midst of an impassioned criticism of Wikipedia, the online publicly written and publicly edited encyclopedia. This librarian was comparing it with the *Britannica* and exhorting students to use only trusted and traditional reference sources.

I don't really want to get bogged down about the accuracy of Wikipedia here, although it is surprisingly accurate. However, the *Britannica* is a nineteenth-century creation, a product of the widespread movement to organize and classify information, pinning it down a little like the beetles and butterflies that nineteenth-century naturalists took pride in skewering to display boards. In fact, biological classification had its roots with Linnaeus, whose system was fine-tuned in the nineteenth century. In chemistry, the periodic table was devised in 1869. We librarians have a fascinating heritage in this regard, and one of the most interesting courses I've ever taken was a history of library classification systems. We are most familiar with Melvil Dewey, but throughout the nineteenth and early twentieth centuries there was a passionate effort underway to organize all knowledge into a neat, orderly bibliographic universe.

The Information Society

Then, of course, the computer arrived and nothing will ever be the same again. We still seek to organize human knowledge, but it has exploded to the point that it is no longer possible to keep it under the control of any small group of well-meaning people. In Wikipedia, we can best view this brave new world of the twenty-first century. I just checked, and Wikipedia tells me it has 3,640,695 articles, 23,987,183 pages, 14,585,766 contributors, and 1,789 administrators. This just isn't the same animal as the *Britannica* and it is not a product of the same worldview. Pining for the old days when knowledge could be neatly organized by officially designated authorities may be tempting, but it is a temptation we must not allow ourselves to fall into. If libraries are to survive, they must be firmly rooted in this world and this time, not in some bygone era.

The computer age has changed society in an infinite number of ways, some good and some bad. The recent populist uprisings in Arab countries, largely made possible by social networking sites like Facebook and Twitter, are evidence that citizens of the Internet do not think highly of authority in any form. And the democratic vision of Wikipedia is right in line with the contemporary mindset. The computer age has brought us many wonderful innovations as well as new causes for concern. However, whatever its strengths or weaknesses, it is the world in which we find ourselves and if we don't want to go the way of the *Britannica*, we'd better get out there and embrace it.

SOCIAL NETWORKING

If librarians have been caught totally off-guard by any revolutionary occurrence in the twenty-first century, it is certainly the development of social networking. Although librarians may possess good or even excellent computer skills, many seem to live and work in a very different world from their customers. The *real-time Web* is a term that describes the many social activities conducted online, including tweets, Facebook status updates and news sharing (think social network icons beside every news article). This face of the Internet is what might be called the successor of Web 2.0, which has been around for several years and appears to be declining in popularity. I discovered in talking with some librarians that they still think Web 2.0 is cutting-edge stuff, and there's a lot to be said for the innovations it brought with it. However, the growing acceptance of smart mobile devices is creating a lucrative market for new real-time apps that are making the Web seem just a little out of date.

The Connected Student

Perhaps it might be useful to describe the networked world through the eyes of one college student. To a large extent, this world is shared by most young people and many adults. The college student I have in mind attends a large university. When she's on campus, she carries with her a "smart" cell phone, in other words a phone that can access the Internet, receive e-mail, send text messages, and link her with Twitter and other social networking services. She has her iPad with her that also allows her to access the Internet wherever she can find a Wi-Fi connection.

Abbie manages to remain in touch with her friends throughout the day. In fact, there are no more than brief periods when she is out of contact. As she walks across campus, she uses Twitter to tell friends where she is going, and she receives brief text messages from other friends who are also checking in. When she arrives at class or the library, she logs into her iPad, clicks on Facebook or Google+, and checks for new messages on her "wall." After quickly responding with her own status update, she transfers her attention to her class or library assignment, but she is never out of contact with her social network. Text and Twitter messages continue to arrive and the Facebook app on her phone adds chats to the conversational mix. Abbie can choose to ignore them all if she doesn't want to be distracted, but she would never consider breaking off the contact. Though not perhaps as often, Abbie also checks her friends' blogs, messages her boyfriend on Google Talk, and continues to check in now and then at her old MySpace page. Her iPad is equipped with a webcam so she can use her Skype account for video phone calls.

The Challenge of Multitasking

If you're a librarian over the age of fifty, your first reaction may be a critical one. "How can she possibly get anything done?" As a profession, we've always been sympathetic to younger generations. We've never concluded that teenagers were going to the dogs and we genuinely enjoy our younger customers. However, many of us just cannot get our heads around social networking. I'm increasingly convinced (and I'm definitely in the over-fifty crowd) that we must become comfortable in this brave new world or we will lose our access to a whole generation.

Abbie is a successful student. She gets mainly A's and B's and enjoys her classes. She has learned to multitask, shifting rapidly from one train of thought to another. As you might expect, the emergence of social networking has given birth to a plethora of research studies, attempting to discover how our brains deal with the complex virtual environment. Although the jury is still out, it does appear that rapid multitasking is more difficult than many young people think and there is some downtime while the brain "changes channels." For some students already experiencing learning difficulties, multitasking may pose yet another challenge. However, multitasking also appears to "stretch" the brain in a positive way, so we'll just have to wait to see how the millennial generation differs from its predecessors. In the meantime, librarians must understand that if they wish to reach their customers, they're going to have to become part of their world.

THE REAL-TIME WEB AND THE REAL-TIME LIBRARY

Assuming that all of us really do want to reach out to our customers, where do we start? How can we plug our libraries into the network so that they become part of Abbie's and her whole generation's virtual world? To start with, we ask

Abbie and her fellow students. We identify those sites in cyberspace where they spend their time. We do not purchase social networking software designed for librarians. We do not enter the virtual world without understanding the rules and customs of social networking. Library literature is chock full of articles about largely unsuccessful projects that involve making the library more computer savvy, usually taking a traditional library service and retooling it for the online environment. Virtual reference is a good example. Librarians have purchased chat programs that both customers and librarians found clunky and intimidating. Other libraries have made electronic reference kiosks available throughout the library without considering that they can be intimidating and hard to use. In essence, we have marked out our territory in cyberspace as, for example, some libraries have re-created themselves in Second Life. Then we've waited and wondered why no one comes to visit us.

How Is the Real-Time Web Different?

As mentioned above, the real-time Web is rapidly replacing the Web as we have come to know it. Perhaps the real-time library needs to become the way we define our online presence. Steven Bell, associate university librarian at Temple University, blogs on *ACRLog*, a site maintained by the Association of College and Research Libraries. I came across one of his posts some time ago and it has continued to occupy my thoughts. Bell attempts to describe how the real-time library differs from the traditional library, and his points hit the mark so well that I have listed them below:

- The real-time library is socially networked but it's about more than just owning social network accounts; the real-time library has an active presence and shares information in real time.
- The real-time library updates its status regularly.
- The real-time library offers targeted services to the networked community.
- The real-time library is accessible on real-time communication devices.
- The real-time library is ready and waiting—all the time—to deliver information services.
- The real-time library monitors the multitude of emerging real-time web services and experiments to find those with the potential to enhance service in real-time mode.
- The real-time library designs information services specifically for delivery and use on the real-time web.
- Real-time librarians are adept at creating relationships with real-time library users.[1]

Social Networking Is a Long-Term Commitment
Even libraries that have been "trendy" enough to create a presence/profile on Facebook or Google+ often get it wrong. It may be a good idea that never really goes anywhere. Perhaps a young library staff member was given the job of maintaining the page when she had a little time on her hands. After the newness wore off, other duties beckoned and the human presence ceased to be present. Naturally, we librarians want to feel cool, and currently nothing is more cool than social networking. Perhaps an idea was hatched in a library meeting without clearly articulated ownership or commitment. Perhaps a computer technician put together a page profile with a photo of the library, and some pictures of studious library users sitting at library computers or lounging in the new books area. Librarians contributed paragraphs about how up-to-date and friendly the library is. However, no sustained effort was made to advertise the profile or attract friends. The wall remained empty of all but a few hearty comments from the library staff. No two-way conversation between staff and customers took place because even if customers wrote comments, staff never saw them.

By the time you read these words, Facebook and Google+ may be passé; Twitter may be in decline. Change happens in the virtual world at breathtaking speed. New online applications appear every month or two, some catching on with the public and some disappearing without a trace. Libraries must be there; they must be where their customers are and be ready to move on when their customers discover their next social networking tool that fits their needs better than the ones they are currently using.

Successful Social Networking Experiences
Since I can't look into a crystal ball and anticipate future applications, I'll tell you a little about what some libraries are doing as this book goes to press. First, they've made a commitment. They are willing to put time, money, and staff resources into their online presence. Their staffs understand the importance of social networking, and some staff members have become expert at maintaining a lively interactive presence. They have large numbers of Facebook friends and know how to create active Google+ circles and hangouts. They send out the most interesting tweets, maintain the most entertaining blogs, and make sure that day in and day out, the library is there with new ideas and appropriate messages (the right length, the right frequency, the right topics).

They understand that in addition to the huge mega-sites like Facebook, there are hundreds of niche sites that appeal to specific groups and they know which ones are especially attractive to their customers. They have a web presence on multiple social networking sites, add content or messages often, and regularly analyze usage statistics to be sure they are reaching the largest number of customers possible. Although they constantly update and improve the library's own website, providing numerous links to and from social networking sites, they do not assume that their customers will come to them without a lot of encouragement. As social networking destinations lose popularity, library staff spend less time on them but they check with their customers to be sure they're making the right choices.

In fact, these libraries are committed to checking in constantly with their customers to find out if they're doing it right. They encourage feedback; they promote real conversation and honest comment. They know how to use and control the medium, using appropriate settings to discourage pranksters and making sure customers can chat with both library staff and one another without being overwhelmed with other content.

Planning a Social Networking Presence

So what might you include on Google+ or the library's Facebook page? Here are some possibilities:

- Ask customers to recommend and review books, DVDs, or magazines for the library's collection (not on a form but simply as one friend sharing information with another).
- Ask their opinion when the library is making decisions.
- Provide portals to other sites for different groups of customers. These can include a wide variety of useful or enjoyable sites that staff members and friends have discovered.
- Provide direct links to library resources so that customers needn't leave the comfort of their favorite site.
- Announce the arrival of new books and media that might be especially popular.
- Encourage customers to comment on local or campus events (be sure you have a usage policy that excludes profanity, pornography, and personal attack).
- Get out information about important local issues with links to more extensive coverage.
- When something especially good or especially bad happens, provide opportunities for the library community to come together and share its feelings.

Attracting Cyber Customers

Even though I began my career as a reference librarian, I feel a lot of trepidation giving advice for creating a popular online reference service. I keep looking for an answer, a model for a program that attracts a large number of library users and is so helpful and enjoyable to use that they sing the library's praises and come back with more questions. What I find are generally library websites that include a text box with a message like "Ask a question" or more specifically "Ask the reference librarian a question." Some sites include a little verbiage about how happy the staff is to be of service. In most cases, if the questions are routed to the right people, the few patrons who take advantage of the service can be accommodated easily and they probably get pretty good answers to their questions within a more or less reasonable time frame. Occasionally, a grad student discovers a sympathetic librarian and an ongoing relationship is established. Mostly, however, the service is little more than a bullet point in the library's annual report, a small attempt to convince board members and administrators that the library isn't an anachronism.

The biggest problem, of course, is that very few users visit the library's website and the few who do are looking for links to the library's catalog or databases. Once they find them, they may well bookmark the specific URL and avoid the library website all together. Since we have considerable evidence that our users are unlikely to come upon the library website but stand a good chance of being logged into Facebook, Google+, or Twitter, these seem like the obvious places to set up our virtual reference desk. In a very short time, other social networking sites will replace them and the online community will become much more fragmented. However, at this moment in time, we can theoretically find many of our users congregating at these cyber destinations.

Attracting Fans and Followers
How will they find us? That's the big problem. Practically every library is experimenting with social networking, but you can see by the number of fans or followers that they are no more successful than they were attracting visitors to the library website. The individuals charged with responsibility for social networking must know what they are doing. They must be avid users of these services or they will be unaware of the reasons why one online presence attracts a thousand fans and another limps along with just a few stalwarts. These first tentative steps that libraries have taken to become part of the social networking scene make one thing painfully clear. If you build it, they will not come. Too many libraries have gone through the motions and found that their efforts just didn't pay off. There are insider rules that must be understood, and the staff members or student assistants who have successful personal networks stand a better chance of creating one for the library.

Since the average reference librarian does not normally spend his day in the socially networked community, he needs guidance and support from someone who does. It clearly takes a team to make it work, so structuring that team is perhaps the most important key to cyber success. Of course, the two worlds occasionally come together in the same person, and this will be increasingly true in the future. However, for now a team seems like the best way to go. I've seen successful projects in which a young adult group teams up with the young adult librarian and college students work closely with the college reference librarian. One very good Facebook page is maintained by an intern who gets input from the entire library staff and serves as a kind of go-between. Whatever the specific arrangement, the factors that determine success seem to be commitment and bona fide social networking credentials.

Informal Language of Cyberspace

Language is something to consider carefully when planning for your online presence. The language of the Internet is informal. Abbreviations are common, and verbal shortcuts help speed up the pace. I've discovered some great library Facebook pages, and it seems clear that tone and choice of words have a lot to do with their success. I'm thinking, for example, of the way one library celebrated the arrival of a new electronic resource. It was obvious that the page was maintained by hip librarians whose informal comments fit in perfectly with those of their "friends." However, it was also clear that there were some colorful expressions that were off-limits. I laughed when the great new resource was referred to as a "kick fanny" database. On the other hand, I've found library Facebook pages that were no more than a reworking of a boring web page.

Social Networking and the Library Staff

Social networking is a personal experience. Users are accustomed to texting or chatting or messaging with an individual, not an institution. That personal quality is missing from many library sites. It may be that librarians are not accustomed to putting themselves forward or sharing personal information with their customers. Privacy and safety considerations also limit what we share about ourselves. Most messages and comments should at least bear the first name of the staff members who wrote them. Customers will go out of their way to seek out the staff member they know both in cyberspace and in the library building. For many of them, the online environment is familiar and comfortable; the library is formal and intimidating.

This brings up the subject of profiles and social networking accounts for individual library staff members. We certainly don't want strangers accessing our personal information on Facebook or Google+. So how can they find us in our library personas? It's interesting to see the creative solutions some librarians have found to this problem. For example, at one library I discovered, staff members have their own Facebook accounts, but their profiles focus on their library interests and responsibilities, not their personal lives. Because they frequently have a separate personal Facebook account, they do not use their full names in their library profile. For example, one may be listed as Susan at Madison Library or perhaps a nickname. The library's site encourages customers to select their own personal librarian, points them to individual profile pages, and encourages them to leave comments and questions.

Blog vs. Website

Libraries face something of a conundrum when they set up shop online. On the one hand, the library website should be extremely well designed. It should have plenty of pizzazz and get customers to the resources they want as quickly and efficiently as possible. It usually takes a web professional to put together a really good website and it is usually very time-consuming. This means that library websites tend to remain frozen, discouraging updates and interaction with customers. On the other hand, the library is a vital, rapidly changing place with news breaking daily and lots of interaction between staff and customers. Social networking sites are designed to accommodate just such activity, but many of the library's customers are not Facebook or Google+ members. If they are to encounter the library online, it may have to be through the library's website. Library blogs that connect seamlessly with the website are a good solution. If done right, library customers are usually completely unaware that they are moving back and forth between website and blog. WordPress and Blogger are two popular online blogging services. In some libraries, a small group of staff members is responsible for the blog. Because blogging applications are almost as easy to use as a word processor, there's usually no need for a computer technician or web professional to be involved.

Specialized Library Apps

By the way, libraries are sometimes offered blogging and other social networking programs as part of their integrated library system (ILS). ILS software, like so many library-focused computer applications, has a relatively small market. Blogger (owned by Google) and WordPress each have millions of user accounts. They are thriving commercial enterprises. Both are top-of-the-line in terms of ease of use and professional-looking results. Like Facebook with its half-billion members, they can afford to hire top programmers and designers. This can't, of course, be said for library software providers. Because the library market is small and not especially profitable, library software tends to be glitchy and idiosyncratic.

Just as OPAC search engines are somewhat primitive when compared to Google, so too social networking applications provided by library vendors can make the library look just a little backward to savvy customers. We don't need to invent our own online universe. Whenever possible, it's better to share the one already inhabited by our customers. Sometimes the popular, mainstream program doesn't really fit our needs, but more often we fall victim to the marketing claims of library vendors. Yes, these programs may make life a little easier on the library end, but how do our customers feel about them? Inevitably, the market for these products is small, and so beta testing is limited. The last thing we want is for our library customers to become unwilling guinea pigs!

Though we have to confess that we're somewhat slow learners when it comes to social networking, we are making progress. There seems to be little question that we were not prepared for this societal transformation, but there truly is a place for us in this brave new world. We must, however, make a real commitment and retool our skills to become successful social networkers. There are few shortcuts and little room for LIS professionals who don't quite approve of this new, networked lifestyle.

NOTE

1. Steven Bell, "The Real-Time Library," *ACRLog,* August 25, 2009, http://acrlog. org/2009/08/25/the-real-time-library/.

RESOURCES

Anttiroiko, A. V., et al. "Towards Library 2.0: The Adoption of Web 2.0 Technologies in Public Libraries." *Libri* 61, no. 2 (June 2011): 87–99.

Connolly, M., et al. "Mobilizing the Library's Web Presence and Services: A Student-Library Collaboration to Create the Library's Mobile Site and iPhone Application" [part of special issue "Mobile Reference: Papers from the Handheld Librarian Conferences"]. *Reference Librarian* 52, no. 1/2 (January/June 2011): 27–35.

Kim, Y. M. "Users' Perceptions of University Library Websites: A Unifying View." *Library & Information Science Research* 33, no. 1 (January 2011): 63–72.

O'Connor, L., et. al. "The Impact of Social Marketing Strategies on the Information Seeking Behaviors of College Students." *Reference & User Services Quarterly* 50, no. 4 (Summer 2011): 351–65.

5 WILL THE COFFEE SHOP SAVE US?

THE LIBRARY AS PLACE

As the demand for printed books and other non-digital library materials declines, the need to simply provide a "place to be" is becoming increasingly important. In the days before computers made their appearance and the vacuum cleaner represented the height of high tech, the world was very different. In 1950, for example, the U.S. population numbered roughly 150,000,000. According to the 2010 census, the population of the United States has risen to about 305,000,000. This means that there are more than twice as many people sharing the same amount of space. In 1950, a much larger portion of the population lived in small towns and rural areas. Now, we are more likely to live in densely populated metropolitan areas. Of course, community services and institutions have grown too, but they have not really kept up with our rapidly expanding population.

OUR CROWDED WORLD

In past years, college students were more likely to attend small private colleges. If they were enrolled in public universities, their world was still a rather small one since the giant institutions that now number students in the tens of thousands were still far in the future. The idea that a lecture hall could hold 500 seats would have seemed preposterous. In those years that marked the start of the baby boom, schoolchildren still attended small schools in their own neighborhoods and classes were similarly small. If they hailed from the midsection of the country, many of today's boomers and seniors remember high school graduating classes not much larger than twenty-five students. Most women worked at home and spent a great deal of time volunteering their services to provide activities (i.e., places to go) for their offspring. Teen clubs flourished and younger children enjoyed a wide variety of supervised after-school activities. Women themselves had their own places to go. Women's service clubs flourished and even "downtown" was still a rather personal space.

Perhaps one of the reasons there are now fewer places to be is that space has become so expensive. With more people needing more space, it is inevitable that spaces not producing income are disappearing. Think, for example, of hotel lobbies. They were once grand spaces in which their guests could spend time enjoying the ebb and flow of humanity. Hotels might even have their own small libraries to entertain their guests. Today's lobby has been reduced to the bare essentials. Most of the space on the main floor is devoted to restaurants and conference rooms, both of which can be used only by people willing to pay for them.

CHANGES IN SOCIETY

The term *soccer mom* has become popular in political parlance to describe women voters who spend their days shuttling their children from activity to activity. However, although children's soccer has gained in popularity over the past fifty years, participation in most organized sports like Little League has declined. Such activities require that a parent be available to pick up children from school and take them to wherever the activity is taking place. When one considers the number of mothers in the workforce and their typical long-distance commutes, it becomes clear that for most soccer moms, supporting their children's recreational activities must be squeezed into the few hours when they are neither sleeping nor working nor getting to and from work.

Other societal changes have made everyone, both young and old, feel less secure. When we imagine the past, we may think of Tom Sawyer or Huckleberry Finn living exciting lives almost completely free of adult supervision. Although these are fictional characters, most children had more freedom back then, and your own parents probably regaled you with their own hair-raising adventures. A child of ten was probably allowed to roam freely until mealtime if there was no work to be done, and parents might see them only now and then. Today, most parents are reluctant to give their children such unrestricted freedom and may tell them to stay at home or call them frequently on their cell phones to report their whereabouts. In many places, walking after dark is unsafe for anyone. Children's outdoor play is restricted, and parents may fear that drug dealers and sexual predators hang out even in better neighborhoods.

Absence of Public Facilities

Another practical difficulty encountered by people looking for something to do is the relative absence of public restrooms and drinking fountains in public places. Town squares once boasted impressive stone drinking fountains that have long since ceased to function. Public restrooms in parks and other places attracted vandals and criminals so they too were shut down. What these societal changes mean is that many people of all ages have few options when it comes to choosing a place to be. There's home, school, work, and perhaps the mall, although malls are usually located off high-speed expressways, not within walking distance of home. College students have their dorm rooms and large impersonal campuses whose facilities are likely to be closed evenings and weekends. Single adults, a growing segment of the population, are busy at work during the day. However, unless they are active churchgoers or social butterflies, they may have little more to do with their leisure hours than watch television and do their laundry. The recession that has gripped the country for several years has had the effect of further reducing leisure options since, for many, discretionary income has been sharply reduced. Seniors have more time on their hands and they typically live alone. As the baby boomers grow older, they will have more time and fewer places to go or activities to occupy them.

NEW ROLES FOR THE LIBRARY

It seems obvious that libraries can fill a number of these needs, but it's hard to know precisely which ones are the best fit. With tight budgets and staff with more than enough to do, how can a library meet pressing societal needs, increase its customer base, and strengthen its bargaining power with local government or its parent institution? This last point is an important one. Few university administrators or county commissioners view the library as having a central role in twenty-first-century society. In fact, they may view the library's usefulness as past and see the library's future as a gradual winding down. This view is widely held by decision-makers in academic institutions, as is discussed in chapter 8. Neither do most school administrators envision their libraries expanding their scope or their services in the future. It may be that public libraries have somewhat more freedom to reinvent themselves, but bringing local officials on board will be no easy task. Thus most libraries will be facing a dual challenge. They must better understand their user community's needs and bet on the right services without wasting too much of their own resources on unsuccessful ventures. In addition, they must somehow manage to convince decision-makers that they need to use this time and some of their funds to gamble on new services at a time when they are being pressured to reduce expenditures.

How People Use the Library

Perhaps it would be helpful to examine why people might wish to merely spend time in the library. I'm not talking about attending the book club or meeting with the Friends of the Library, although those are certainly enjoyable pastimes. I mean simply sitting at a table or in a lounge chair and just being there. The homes of most people (I'm excluding the McMansions of the rich) are getting smaller. For many years, home size kept steadily increasing. Then came the recession and the trend sharply changed direction. Nationally, the average home size is predicted to decrease 10% by 2015. In the crowded northeastern United States, house size shrank by more than 200 square feet in a single year.

Families downsized their living space when money got tight, and larger homes became less popular with buyers. The National Association of Home Builders conducted a survey of builders and reported that most are planning to build smaller homes for the foreseeable future. Builders of smaller homes may be rewarded with coveted LEED low-energy certificates that further encourage the building of smaller homes. This is great for the environment, but it may be hard on people who must spend too many hours looking at their own four walls.

While home size has been shrinking, the recession has caused family size to increase. Although this may be a temporary trend, extended families with multiple generations living together have become more common. Since the unemployment rate is much higher among younger adults, many twenty-somethings are returning home to live with mom and dad. This may be great for family bonding, but both older and younger generations may need to get away from all that togetherness.

Responding to the Need for a Place to Be

The spaciousness of the library can be very enticing when one has spent the day in a cramped 600-square-foot condo or camping out in the basement of one's family home. Nevertheless, when library acreage is filled with range after range of dusty old books, the sense of spaciousness dissolves. The space may also fail to charm if the library does not appeal to the five senses. Think about the places that you enjoy. They tend to be large, open, and airy. However, a space that's too large seems impersonal, institutional rather than human-size. The ideal is a balance of the two, a place where we feel cozy and comfortable, out of the way of foot traffic. We are cheered by sunlight, prefer a comfortable room temperature without drafts, and want to be in places that are free from unpleasant odors and loud noises. Dampness, glare, dust, and uncomfortable furniture can also turn what might have been an enjoyable place to be into a place we want to leave. All of this means that simply having a large space available does not ensure that we will automatically attract customers to the library.

Most libraries are experiencing some decline in traditional print circulation and can anticipate further drops as customers purchase more e-book readers. At the same time, appealing "places to be" are disappearing. If we consider these trends together, we find we have some unique opportunities to rethink library space utilization. Naturally, we want to make the best use of the opportunity, both because we want the library to be relevant to our communities and also because we want to keep our jobs.

Nevertheless, this change in the way people use the library poses new challenges. Of course, we've always served a variety of customer needs and our visitors have looked to the library as a place to be. However, we have tended to concentrate our efforts on those customers who come to the library, select a few best sellers, DVDs, or children's books and leave. Let's take a moment to consider how the needs of this group differ from those of people who are not coming for "things" but for an experience. This group may look at a library in much the same way as they might a movie theater. They're coming for entertainment, for diversion, and to enrich the quality of their lives. This is a tall order!

The Library as an Experience

Ideally, these experience-seekers might spend an hour or two browsing through the new books, reading a chapter here and there. If they're news junkies, they may devour not only the local newspaper but regional and national newspapers as well. Then they may check their e-mail on a library computer or on their own laptop. Although most people who use the library's Wi-Fi network don't have a high-speed connection at home, some use the library just to be around other people. They will all need chairs that are comfortable enough that they can enjoy a relaxing experience. The elderly, as well as the aging baby boomer population, will require seating that is not only comfortable but kind to the sacroiliac. Longer visits mean heavier restroom use and, consequently, a heavier workload for custodians.

The term *grazing* has been borrowed from the farm to describe the contemporary approach to eating. Increasingly, people tend to divide the consumption of the day's calories among a number of small snacks, rather than compressing them into three larger meals. They also enjoy combining eating with other activities like reading, listening to music, and watching television. Librarians of the past tended to consider such behavior as almost decadent. Food and drink did not belong in the library and that was that. Today's more socially aware staff members have accepted this new reality, but they may be unsure about how the library should respond. No matter what the type of library, print materials are usually retained for only a few years. Google, interlibrary loan, and full-text periodical databases have all had the effect of limiting most library collections to recent publications plus a small rare book, special collections, or local history area.

Focusing on the Building

Thus, preservation issues have declined in importance in most libraries. However, wear and tear on carpet and furniture increases rapidly when customers treat the library like their living rooms. In general, the kinds of construction and decorating materials that resist stains, gouges, and breakage are those found in airports. Like cement, stone, and tile, they are hard, cold, and unyielding. They do not invite our customers to choose the library as a favorite place to be.

Therefore, the decision to provide the kind of environment that will attract customers necessitates a complex plan for maintaining the library. Furniture must be cleaned, repaired, or replaced on a regular schedule. Spot cleaning to attack stains while they can still be removed must become everyone's job. Carpet tiles should probably replace broadloom, and custodial services must become just as important and highly respected as any library department.

Library directors and other staff members need to have a role in selecting the materials used in decorating and equipping the library, and they also need to understand the properties of each. Sanitation, germ control, and air filtration all affect customer satisfaction and well-being, so they must become important to us. That means we must develop and enforce policies that are sensitive to the needs of the homeless and mentally ill but require acceptable hygiene practices to use the library. None of this is new. Maintaining our buildings has always been part of our jobs, but we can expect that tomorrow's library building will require more expertise and attention. I, for one, never had a course in library school that taught me about building maintenance. Though always understood to be part of the job, it was a rather lowly part, not one that required a great deal of professional expertise. If, however, we want libraries to survive and prosper, our attitudes are going to have to undergo a sea change.

A Place No One Wants to Be

As I write, I can't help but think of a major university library I visited. Recently renovated and expanded, it is considerably larger than most academic libraries and boasted an unusually generous capital outlay budget. Nevertheless, the result is a place where few people would wish to spend much of their time. Probably intending to staff the library more efficiently and provide better security, architects designed the space with an absolute minimum of separate rooms or room dividers. With the exception of offices, workspaces, restrooms, and collaborative studies, each floor consisted of one vast, open space. Book stacks, often compact shelving units, have been placed around the perimeter of the space. A vast reading area occupies the center. Every floor is almost identical to every other floor and one color has been used throughout. By the time I had completed my tour, I was thoroughly sick of that color. Walls, carpeting, and furniture must have been special orders because they all matched exactly. Every table matched every other table, every chair was identical in every way to every other chair. Whether you were tall or short, fat or slim, you sat in the same chair. Whatever your personal needs and preferences, whatever kind of space you found appealing, you had no choice.

However, it was the sense of vastness that was most disconcerting. I have frequently watched library customers choose their table or study carrel. They will first look around to see what is available. Then they will select either a window seat if it is a sunny day or a nook where they can feel cozy. Of course, access to electric outlets may play a role in the decision, but a table in the middle of a large room is rarely a customer's first choice. I'm not sure of the psychological reasons behind their decisions, but perhaps they feel exposed and unprotected. The library I'm describing has no nooks, no personal spaces, and very few tables or carrels placed near windows. In fact, it seems that customers' preferences played no role at all in the placement of the library's windows.

Both Comfort and Security

We all understand that security is an increasingly important concern. With library staffs getting smaller, we are naturally worried about the safety of our customers. Of course, we don't want to create isolated rooms or long corridors where miscreants can molest people without being heard or seen. However, security cameras have become standard in most libraries and once the system is in place, individual cameras are cheap. It is possible to create lots of comfortable places that give visitors some sense of personal space without endangering them. No one expects complete privacy in a library and most don't want it. Typically customers want to be near enough to strangers to sense their presence but not so near that they become intrusive.

I admit that I can get lost easily, but the library discussed here seems deliberately designed to be as confusing as possible. Visitors to this library have almost no visual cues to guide them through the building. One wall looks like another. Banks of stacks may be designated by discreet signage, but one quickly loses one's sense of direction. Since walls, carpet, furnishings, and signs were designed to match one another and everything was purchased in huge quantities, there are no landmarks to help you get your bearings, and few bright pops of color from large artworks or attractive graphics capture your attention. It is only at the elevators that you can find other colors, but the elevators are located in a small, nearly invisible alcove.

It's Not Someone Else's Job

Since I did not want to wear out my welcome and I felt my tour guide becoming defensive, I did not ask who designed the interior of the building. However, after visiting many large libraries, I'm convinced that neither the library director nor the library staff had a large part in the planning. It was probably the work of an administrator charged with responsibility for planning the interiors of institutional buildings, working with a design professional or furniture contractor. The library director or her designee signed off on the selections. However, no matter who made the decisions, their goal was to get the job done. It's hard to believe that any thought was given to the needs of the human beings who would use the building.

THE HUMAN SIDE OF THE LIBRARY

If the social networking phenomenon has taught us anything, it is that people need more social interaction than was previously understood. Surveys indicate that most young adults remain in contact with friends and relatives throughout the day via texting, chatting, e-mailing, and instant messaging. It has long been known that the majority of the population are more extroverted than introverted, but interpersonal contact was limited by the demands of daily life. However, with the arrival of each scientific breakthrough, we have found that technical innovations are almost immediately co-opted for social activities. The Internet itself, originally called ARPANET, was developed primarily for defense purposes and to facilitate the exchange of scientific information. Almost immediately, however, researchers created recreational bulletin boards and newsgroups, as well as personal e-mail. It was not anticipated that strangers separated by thousands of miles would seek out one another just to enjoy their virtual company. Neither was it anticipated that cell phone technology would result in a world of individuals who remain constantly connected, no matter whether they are walking to the subway, shopping at the mall, or eating in a restaurant. Facebook and Twitter are the latest manifestations of this reality. Most human beings appear to want to be physically or virtually in touch with others during much of their day.

The Need for Companionship

Yet traditional libraries can be lonely places. People sit alone studying, reading, or viewing media. Of course, to some extent, solitude may be necessary for concentration, but if our customers are to enjoy the library as a place to be, the ability to concentrate on a demanding project may not be a high priority. In fact, the generations that grew up after the introduction of personal computers and portable music players tend to be multitaskers. They may prefer to read while listening to music or text message while studying. On the other hand, people over fifty tend to be turned off by a lot of noise and confusion. Librarians are often members of this latter group and they are sometimes inclined to criticize rather than accommodate multitaskers. Too often, they may seek to make the library the kind of place that meets their own needs but not those of their customers.

Of course, the library can passively accommodate a certain amount of social interaction merely by providing Wi-Fi access. If it goes a step further and provides a generous number of electrical outlets to accommodate personal computers, the library becomes an even more desirable place to recharge both one's laptop battery and one's own personal biological battery. Taking it one step further, customers can be greeted at the entrance with a sign encouraging them to pause, rest for a moment, and log their computers into the library's Facebook page. If the Facebook page leads to an online chat room, they can enjoy the company of other library customers, and feel even more comfortable.

Connecting the Arriving Patron

An unobtrusive librarian or even a student assistant hosting the chat room can answer questions and help orient new arrivals, but customers should also be encouraged to chat with one another. They can check online to see if any of their friends are in the library. Then they can message or text one another as they read or study or use the Internet. Later they can arrange to lunch or take a break together. Since social networking websites and software are "hot," there will be better ways to connect your customers with one another and with the library staff by the time you read this book. The important thing to remember is that your customers do not want to feel alone and isolated. They won't choose a seat in an empty stack or reading area, and they will not remain in the library for very long if they do not have some positive interactions with the staff and the people around them.

Staff Experience the Library Differently

For the most part, members of the library staff are like anyone else, but a number of studies have found that they are somewhat more introverted than their customers. They enjoy being with others, but they are also somewhat more comfortable working alone than is typical of the larger population. Staff are also accustomed to the library and may be unaware of how large, cold, and unfriendly it feels to visitors. Staff know where things are located so they do not experience the frustration of wasting time or the exhaustion of wandering around the building. If you want the library to attract a large number of customers and remain productive and relevant, you must make it a place where many people want to be and where they experience a minimum of discomfort and confusion.

Another thing to consider is how people interact with strangers. As I mentioned, most people draw comfort from being near others whom they don't know, but not too near. For example, a lounge area where visitors can browse new books and newspapers is always popular. It is pleasanter to read the morning newspaper in the company of other people who are doing the same thing. Although some people will try to find a totally private area in which to read, most of us prefer to have a sense that others are nearby as long as they aren't annoying or distracting.

The Need for Personal Space

Generally, we won't share a study table or a sofa with a stranger unless the area is crowded. You might try an experiment that I devised a few years ago. Keep an eye on an area where several people are reading. One by one, they will leave the area and at first the other occupants won't seem to notice. However, when the next to last leaves, the lone remaining reader will look up. In a few minutes, he will get his own things together and leave the area. Of course, this doesn't happen every time, but I've noticed it often enough that it can't be coincidence.

These customers want a certain amount of personal space or separation from one another, and they are uncomfortable when they feel exposed. For example, if this seating group is in the middle of a large open space, they will feel much less comfortable than if a low shelving range separates them from the central high-traffic area. If you are expecting a library renovation or expansion, it might be helpful to design some experiments of your own. Move some chairs closer together and space others farther apart. Which are more popular? Move some chairs out toward the middle of a space and leave others near a wall or stack range. Which chairs get more use? Arrange some sofas so they face each other, and position others so they are at right angles to one another. You can probably think of a lot of different arrangements, but the important thing is to look for patterns and draw inferences from what you observe.

Planning for Individual Preferences

Most libraries offer Wi-Fi access, so customers frequently bring their laptop computers. Obviously, they're going to look for a spot where they can plug into an electric outlet, but what other factors determine their seating preferences? Some years ago, I worked in a library that was experiencing severe financial problems. We desperately needed furniture, and the only place I could get it was at the government surplus center that adjoined the library property. I could buy furniture for next to nothing but items rarely matched. I purchased a large number of mismatched tables and chairs and had them painted a uniform color. There were big chairs and little chairs, soft chairs and hard chairs. In fact, there were even large, adult-size beanbags. Just as library customers sought out the same reading area or the same window, they also developed strong preferences for certain chairs (the beanbags were surprisingly popular).

Creating a Happening Place

If we want our customers to come to the library more frequently, we also need to provide more things for them to do. In recent years, public libraries have done a great job of planning popular library programs. Young adult activities have exploded, and children's summer reading programs encompass more and more interesting and educational activities. Adult programming has become more varied, ranging from Metropolitan Opera simulcasts to African violets to NASCAR auto racing. However, libraries tend to take a shotgun approach to programming, scheduling events because they happen to have a speaker handy but failing to take note of how many customers attended or whether they enjoyed the program.

Libraries also tend to plan many of their programs for the same small group of people. Of course, we must consider our regular customers when we plan events and we know there are certain people we can count on to attend. However, programming gives us an opportunity to serve a broader customer base encompassing different demographic groups. If we advertise in the right way in the right places, we can reach people who might otherwise never visit the library.

I think librarians have always been scrupulously careful about such issues as political balance, but they have tended to develop programs that they themselves might like to attend. Consider the different groups your library is expected to serve. Which ones are not using the library? How might their interests be different from those of your regular customers? In my own Wyoming, cowboy poetry is hot, but cowboy poets aren't usually library users. Savvy Wyoming librarians have learned that the library can become the very epicenter of the cowboy poetry community; it just takes some thinking out of the box. Local government decision-makers may be another group that isn't using the library. I happen to know a fiendishly clever librarian who did some snooping and identified the hobbies and other leisure pursuits of her county commissioners. For some strange reason, her library has hosted a surprising number of programs in those interest areas. Of course, everyone in our community is important, but there is no question that programming can be an effective tool for reeling in library holdouts.

THE CHALLENGE OF THE STAGNATING LIBRARY

Infrequently, a situation arises that can be very dangerous for the professional staff working in a library. Something has caused the library to become stuck in a rut. Perhaps it is a director who, over the years, has lost interest in her job. Perhaps it is a board or a dean who has a very outdated idea of what a library should be. It can even be the staff themselves, who resist all efforts to update their skills and develop new programs. Repeated budget cuts may also make those who labor on behalf of the library feel unappreciated. Whatever the reason, this is a toxic situation, and sooner or later some decision-maker is going to realize that the library isn't worth the money that's going into it and heads are likely to roll.

As the recession has continued, we've seen many public officials and legislators who think they can solve their budget crisis by making some government agency look wasteful and unnecessary. Some libraries have already been their victims and more will find themselves in the crosshairs. What can you do if you know you are working in just such a library and you want to protect both your library and your job? You'll need to initiate change, make the library look good, and keep a low profile. Don't alienate the individuals you consider to be responsible for the problem. On the one hand, you may not understand the constraints they are working under. On the other, you must have their support to pursue your revitalization strategies.

Revitalizing the Dysfunctional Library
Here are a few suggestions for getting your stodgy library moving. (If the situation is bad enough, you may need to jump ship, so while you're revving up the library, be sure to rev up your own resume.)

- Get permission to write a grant proposal for a new program. Most administrators and boards are looking for additional library funding, so it is usually easier to innovate if someone else is providing the funding; Give yourself a specific role in the project and you might even be able to list yourself as project director. Good for your resume and good for the library!
- Research successful new programs in other libraries and pick one that you think you could develop in the time you have available without a major change in your job description. Choose one that will make you look more employable on a resume and might give you a more central role in library planning. Your strategy here will be to introduce the program as quietly and painlessly as possible. Encourage your superiors to bask in the positive feedback. Once they buy into it, see if you can begin altering your title or job description around the program.
- Control the image of the library in the minds of customers and decision-makers. Start a newsletter or other public relations (PR) initiative. Decide what you want to emphasize and what you want to keep mum about. In essence, you are creating the library as you want it to be.
- Stuck-in-a-rut libraries tend to collect a lot of statistics and file them away. Find ways to use them for PR but be selective. Skip over downward trends if possible and concentrate on big numbers like attendance. Again, think of the image you are creating and be careful how you sculpt it.
- Get buy-in from colleagues. They too are in danger if negative attention is focused on the library. Partner with other staff members on projects. Make sure they get plenty of credit.

If tomorrow's libraries are to be popular places where many people come to spend their time, then we must view those customers as individuals. They will come to the library if the library meets their needs; in other words, if it provides information and entertainment, delights their senses, and allows them to enjoy the company of other people. Future technology will, of course, impact libraries, but it's hard to imagine that any twenty-first-century discovery or innovation will have more impact on our future well-being than simply providing a place to be.

RESOURCES

Breeding, M. "Using Technology to Enhance a Library as Place." *Computers in Libraries* 31, no. 3 (April 2011): 29–31.

Gerke, J., et al. "The Physical and the Virtual: The Relationship between Library as Place and Electronic Collections." *College & Research Libraries* 71, no. 1 (January 2010): 20–31.

Griebel, R. "The Library as Place in California." *Feliciter* 55, no. 2 (2009): 65, 70.

Mardis, M. A. "Reflections on School Library as Space, School Library as Place." *School Libraries Worldwide* 17, no. 1 (January 2011): I–III.

Montgomery, S. E., et al. "The Third Place: The Library as Collaborative and Community Space in a Time of Fiscal Restraint." *College & Undergraduate Libraries* 18, no. 2/3 (April–September 2011): 228–38.

Van Vuren, A. J., et al. "Is the Hybrid Library the Future Destination of Choice?" *Mousaion* 27, no. 2 (2009): 1–16.

Young, S. "Looking Beyond the Stacks: The Law Library as Place." *AALL Spectrum* 14, no. 9 (July 2010): 16–19, 21.

6

LIBRARY
CAREERS THAT
WON'T GO AWAY

As dedicated LIS professionals, we are all vitally interested in the future of libraries, but we must admit that we have a personal prejudice when approaching the subject. This is our profession. We have committed a sizeable part of our lives to our libraries and we are not only interested in their well-being but in our own as well. In the brave new world of the future, will there continue to be librarians as we understand the term? Are we an endangered species? Should we abandon ship and prepare ourselves for a different profession? What are our options?

THE MARKET VALUE OF LIS SKILLS

A friend recently confessed that she had earned an MLIS degree years ago but had never worked in a library. She had discovered that computer programmers, systems analysts, and other information technology (IT) professionals earn a lot more than librarians, and her LIS background served as an excellent basis on which to build a computer science career. Hers is not an unusual story. If you begin with the skills at which librarians typically excel, those that involve organizing and accessing information, then add technical courses, and top it all off with a master's degree, you probably have a very marketable professional.

Of course, things don't always work this way, but it points out a difficulty that may plague twenty-first-century libraries. In order for libraries to remain relevant and successful, they need professional staff who possess highly marketable qualifications. They seek decision-makers who can take the lead in technological development, rather than stand on the sidelines. However, unlike many other IT professionals, library staff must understand people and their unique needs since the roles of mediator and advocate are central to effective library service. Finally, they must feel such enthusiasm for and dedication to their profession that they are not tempted by the generous salaries paid to other IT professionals.

The Current Job Market

As I write, libraries are experiencing the impact of the "great recession" and despite its negative impact in other respects, libraries are having no difficulty hiring highly qualified staff. Job seekers have few options, and library salaries look good when compared to unemployment. This will soon change, however, as job seekers find themselves more marketable and job openings in every industry become more plentiful. By that time, the impact of massive library retirements will also be felt. Librarians on average are older than members of other occupations. In fact, the average librarian is a woman in her fifties. A report prepared for the American Library Association Senior Management and Executive Board found that 41 percent of the people who identified themselves as librarians on the 2000 census were between 50 and 59 years of age and more than 8 of every 10 were female.[1] Smaller but more recent studies have indicated that the average age is continuing to climb. Baby boomers have long been what might be called our core group and as they age, so does the profession. As boomers retire, new arrivals are not keeping pace. In 2000, 2 percent of library directors were age 65 and over, with the number climbing to 9 percent in 2005 and still continuing to rise each year. There are some differences among types of libraries, but there is no question that a large percentage of the profession has reached or is nearing retirement age.

JOBS FOR THE FUTURE

There is probably no better place to begin evaluating the future viability of our profession than with the U.S. government's *Occupational Outlook Handbook*. As we explain to our users, the job market changes too rapidly for any single reference source to keep up and so information rapidly becomes dated. However, the "Outlook for Librarians" section of the handbook still provides a number of important insights. In the midst of recession, its bureaucratic-sounding conclusion that job growth will be limited by budget constraints strikes us as the ultimate understatement. However, its analysis of employment trends is extremely relevant. For example, it emphasizes that jobs for librarians outside traditional settings will grow fastest over the decade. Nontraditional librarian jobs usually involve working somewhere other than in a library and that includes information brokers, as well as information professionals who work for private corporations, nonprofit organizations, and consulting firms. Again, the recession may impede progress in this direction, since the employers who will hire these information professionals will need some time to recover financially. However, there is no question that sectors like business, law, technology, and medicine need precisely the skills that librarians possess.

Jobs Outside the Library

It may seem surprising, but the *Occupational Outlook Handbook* has especially positive things to say about archivists, librarians' sister profession in the LIS family. Archival services are undergoing a resurgence of vitality. In particular, digital archives have ushered in a new and exciting era. In the past, openings for archivists have been limited and competition has been keen. At present, there are a large number of qualified applicants for most positions. However, we are told that employment of archivists, curators, and museum technicians will increase 20 percent over the next decade, a considerably higher rate than in most other occupations. Of course, state and local government units will take time to recover. Their current spending is based on last year's tax collections. This means that they are always behind the private-sector economy. Archivists who specialize in electronic records and records management will find they are much more marketable than archivists whose experience is concerned exclusively with older media formats. In fact, all across the LIS spectrum, professionals who are successful at marrying traditional information skills with sophisticated technical know-how will find themselves highly employable.

After the Economy Recovers

Nevertheless, libraries will probably continue to be the main employers of information professionals, so the next question that confronts us is which type of library offers the brightest prospects for the future. Of course, every library is currently experiencing major challenges, but the great unknown is how they will emerge when the economy rebounds. Each type has endemic problems that won't completely disappear when funding becomes more plentiful. For example, academic libraries are experiencing some declines in usage that are likely to continue no matter what the state of the economy. The battle that is currently being waged between e-book publishers and libraries may be related to the economy, but money alone will not lead to a friendly reconciliation. The online availability of other library resources will play an especially important role in the future of brick-and-mortar libraries.

Although school libraries are also experiencing competition from online resources, other forces are impacting the futures of school library professionals. For example, school librarians earn teaching credentials and are paid salaries roughly equivalent to those of classroom teachers. They will continue to have an uphill battle convincing school boards and the general public that their positions are needed as much as the teachers who might be hired in their place. While academic librarians find support in tough accreditation standards, school libraries have not been so successful and have lost out in some important accreditation decisions. Public library use tends to rise during a recession because fewer people have money for expensive leisure pursuits and so are more likely to take advantage of the wealth of free services offered by libraries. Unfortunately, this means that the need is highest when library resources are being stressed to the limit. When budgets are tight, it is not uncommon for local governments and library boards to question the need for professional positions that are not supervisory in nature.

Is LIS an Underrated Profession?

No matter what the type of library, it suffers from the common disadvantage that decision-makers are not heavy users of its services. For example, students usually have little power to impact the library budget. In the corporate world, top managers do not prepare their own reports. Decision-makers may be unaware that much of the information provided by administrative assistants and lower-level managers is actually supplied by librarians. It does appear, however, that special librarians are becoming much more savvy about documenting and marketing their accomplishments. Studies confirm that there is a direct relationship between the research, organizational, and technical expertise provided by librarians and the profitability of businesses. Librarians are able to review huge amounts of information, analyzing, evaluating, and organizing it so that decision-makers can focus their efforts more strategically.

LIS professionals may fail to fully comprehend their potential value to an organization. If they are largely unacquainted with the world outside the library, they may not realize that their combination of talent and education is both valuable and unusual. Professionals like themselves have been successful in positions with titles like systems analyst, web developer, database specialist or trainer, and local area network coordinator. They need not be tied to a library to be successful. In fact, breaking loose and creating new titles and job descriptions for themselves may considerably improve their employment prospects. All of this means that LIS students and new grads may find themselves in a position to invent their jobs if they fully understand where their skills are needed. Internships are an excellent way to learn about the world outside the library. Because interns are not costly, supervisors may be more willing to allow them to experiment, to initiate new services that can make the employer more efficient or profitable. Sometimes, an internship leads to a full-time job. In other situations, the intern is able to identify existing positions and job titles for which she could adapt her skills.

Retooling for the Future

Other LIS professionals are at roughly the midpoint of their careers and wonder whether they should be actively retooling and moving to more marketable specializations. They are different from new grads in that they have a lot invested in their careers. They have been moving up the ladder with steadily rising salaries and increasing responsibility and status. They don't want to start over and yet they fear that their jobs may become obsolete. What should they do? The simple answer in many situations is to stay with the old job but develop new technology skills. They will then be prepared to assume new responsibilities as opportunities arise. That way, their job descriptions can evolve fairly painlessly until eventually it becomes appropriate to change the job title. If these mid-level professionals have been guiding the evolution of their jobs, they are likely to have much more job security than the person who continues to do the same job until decision-makers finally realize it is no longer relevant to the modern library.

Some jobs, however, have been disappearing steadily from libraries and the recession has only hastened the trend. Without a clear plan of how the job can be transformed into one that meets tomorrow's needs, it may not be safe to count on it. In fact, it could be a big mistake to assume that you can safely glide toward retirement without a painful crash along the way. For example, some very interesting things are happening in the world of government documents, but there is no question that fewer libraries feel the need for a documents librarian. Even if these librarians are successful in upgrading their technical skills, the positions themselves may be among the first to be eliminated when funding is tight. Film librarians may also fall into this category. Years ago, catalogers were often the first to use computers in their work, and since almost no one in the library was technically savvy in those days, they often evolved into systems librarians. In today's library, however, such transitions don't happen as often. Systems is a well-established position with a ladder of increasing technical responsibility. Catalogers would do well to take stock and make an objective assessment of their roles. Are they gradually becoming less relevant in their libraries or are they assuming more prominent technology-related roles and responsibilities?

Rebranding for the Future

No matter what your position in the library, you may wish to give some thought to rebranding yourself. If your job title was in use twenty or thirty years ago, it may be time for a makeover. Take, for example, a serials position. The work of the serials librarian was once quite complicated. Discovering when and how a particular journal merged with another, changed its title, and altered the way it numbered its volumes could be a demanding and intellectually stimulating quest. When the Internet and networked cataloging utilities made such information readily available, libraries had the choice of downgrading the position to a paraprofessional one or adding new responsibilities. As we all know, professional positions are hard to come by and most libraries would not willingly reduce their numbers. Therefore, they might choose to keep the position as it was but change the job description.

However, when decision-makers look at a job title that hasn't changed since the days of printed check-in cards, they may not look deeper to discover that the actual job description has remained relevant over the years. Your challenge may be to rebrand yourself with a new job title and some shiny new qualifications. Now is certainly the time to keep a weather eye out for what is happening in your specialty area. Read the job ads even if you are not looking for a job. How many openings do you see with your title? Networking with other librarians can be especially important. Although it might sound a little mean, you might think of them as canaries in a coal mine. If you learn that their jobs are in danger, yours may be next. Those of us who have worked at the same job for many years have difficulty imagining that our libraries can function without us. Then a new director or an edict from on high brings about a complete reorganization. Anyone whose skills and experience do not fit neatly into the new structure is going to have a hard time and so it is better to be prepared.

Job Titles with Legs

Both mid-level LIS professionals and new grads would do well to take a good look at the most popular online job sites and get their tongues (and their brains) around some of those trendy job titles. The following are just a few of the ones I collected on a recent surfing expedition:

- ILS (integrated library system) librarian
- Digital services librarian
- Knowledge access management librarian
- Digital collection services librarian
- E-access and serials librarian
- Electronic access librarian

Bridging the Communication Gap

I'm also going to make up my own name for another very marketable position that requires good technology skills. I think I'll call it *communicator* or *interpreter* or perhaps *go-between*. Technology is absolutely central to the success of today's library no matter what type it may be, but libraries often lack the funding to hire high-level computer professionals. Instead, they tend to hire relatively inexperienced young technicians to maintain their networks and perform the more demanding computer tasks. Thus libraries tend to be divided into two kingdoms. On one side are the older, more experienced staff members who know the ropes and have well-developed work habits. On the other side are the young computer staff who in many ways are typical of entry-level workers anywhere but who hold the fate of the library in their hands. For example, a technician may fail to understand that a computer function is essential to the library's operation, and for several days the library may be paralyzed while an error is corrected.

It is becoming increasingly important for a library to have professionals on its staff who can communicate with both kingdoms. The senseless conflicts that we see in many libraries destroy both the staff's esprit de corps and the confidence that library users place in their libraries. It takes an excellent supervisor to work effectively with a young, inexperienced staff and effectively direct their talents to meet library needs. The job calls for a tremendous amount of patience as well as both well-developed technical skills and solid LIS credentials.

Jobs That Support Tomorrow's Library

In chapter 5, we considered how the library is increasingly becoming a destination for people who simply want "a place to be." It is in the library's interest to encourage this trend, but to do so requires a significant staffing commitment. In fact, we might say that to attract patrons seeking a place to be, the library must take on two commitments. First, of course, is the commitment to maintain the library building itself at a level that will make the library a desirable destination. The custodial staff, of course, has a key role, but an additional commitment is needed. It is important that a staff member be able to bridge the gap between the library user and the "keepers of the library building."

In other words, a manager is needed to identify the ways in which the public uses or wants to use the building and interpret this information to other library staff members. At what time should the restrooms be cleaned so more people can have a clean facility and fewer people are inconvenienced when it is closed for cleaning? Why doesn't the public use the area on the north side of the building? Is it because there's a strong draft coming through the windows? Is there something wrong with the heating? The maintenance staff may be unaware that heat isn't getting to this area because they don't spend time there. The public feels the discomfort but is more likely to find another seating area than report the problem. Someone needs to be responsible for making sure such problems aren't ignored.

Similarly, someone should be responsible for noticing that the blue sofa needs to be replaced or the wall covering in the periodicals area requires repair. The person assigned to such tasks must have a budget and decision-making authority over that budget. He should have the authority to establish priorities that might involve delaying one planned purchase so that a problem affecting a larger number of users can be remedied. In addition, he needs to have some knowledge of furniture construction, the durability of upholstery fabrics, and graffiti-resistant wall coverings.

Changing Definitions for Professional Positions

At first glance, this is a position that does not sound like a professional one. In fact, libraries have traditionally dealt with such problems by tacking duties onto the job description of a secretary or perhaps circulation head. In other words, such duties were afterthoughts. Yet mistakes can be extremely costly, and failure to devote time and energy to such tasks can create widespread customer dissatisfaction. The job I am describing may require more knowledge of furniture construction than digital information resources. What this staff member really does is manage resources and coordinate the overall effort to meet user needs, a very important and complicated job. Not all such positions need to be viewed as professional ones. However, I think that if we don't begin seeing user satisfaction as our highest priority and make it the responsibility of our best and brightest staff, we are going to miss some important opportunities. If we fail to appreciate the importance of such a position, we risk having a professional staff who live in an ivory tower and have little understanding of the needs of the very people they were hired to serve.

During most of the twentieth century, we defined professional positions as those that required the most advanced educational credentials and the highest skill levels. The definition had a practical side; in other words, we wanted people who knew what they were doing running our libraries. However, it was also intended as a way to force the public to look at librarians as professionals and their work as intellectually demanding. Computers, however, have turned job descriptions that were once highly challenging into routine clerical jobs that can be performed by any reasonably competent staff member. Reference work is nothing like it once was, and librarians who expect stimulating reference questions may wait in vain. On the other hand, jobs like the one described above can make or break a library. How do we reconcile the more academic definition of an LIS professional with the reality of the twenty-first-century library? I'm convinced that we must put aside intellectual snobbery and make certain that our most highly qualified staff are the ones who make the important decisions, and those decisions are at least as likely to concern restrooms as access to digital materials.

CHALLENGES FACING LIS EDUCATORS

Just as LIS professionals in the trenches are aging, so too are LIS educators. In fact, our academic programs have taken a beating over the years, with many master's programs closing and others attracting only limited numbers of students. These losses, in turn, limit the number of classes that can be offered, as well as the diversity of course offerings. During the 1960s and '70s, it was thought that there was going to be a shortage of librarians so the federal government made generous scholarships available to PhD students who were intending to teach. They earned their degrees, obtained teaching positions, and once they were granted tenure, they tended to stay in the same jobs for the remainder of their careers. Most LIS faculty work hard to keep up with technology and other twenty-first-century developments, but they do not possess the technical and managerial expertise that recent PhDs could bring to the profession. New blood is in short supply. The recession has further restricted opportunities to expand LIS programs and make them more relevant.

Patching Together a Great LIS Program

I believe it is vital for LIS academic programs to reach out to other departments within their universities to bring much-needed technical and managerial strength into the curriculum. We're simply not going to see legions of young, technically savvy LIS faculty joining the ranks anytime soon, but we must provide the educational experiences that students need. Most of the universities with accredited LIS programs possess precisely the resources that today's professionals need. The problem is that LIS faculty are often ignorant of the courses available in other departments. When students ask to put their own programs together, they usually get a somewhat positive reception but they also encounter a certain amount of departmental territorialism. "Sure, you can take those MBA courses as long as you take all these LIS courses too."

If I could wave my magic wand, I'd bring together LIS faculty, successful practitioners who know what's happening in the real world, and faculty from the academic departments whose offerings can be enormously useful to our graduates. I'd ask them to work out programs of study that really meet the needs of twenty-first-century information professionals. It is unfair to ask students to take on this responsibility because most of them haven't been out there in the trenches and lack the insider knowledge of faculty. They have a right to know that the courses they take will actually prepare them for the future and give them the tools to keep growing in their profession no matter where in the university they're housed. There are, to be sure, some LIS programs that have put together somewhat similar coalitions, but they are certainly not the norm.

At the beginning of this chapter, I asked a question about whether LIS is still a viable career choice. We all want to know whether there are calm seas ahead or if we should abandon a sinking ship. At this point, there seems to be little reason to completely abandon LIS but some changes are inevitable. Since the future is uncertain, we should be prepared for a variety of scenarios. Whatever happens, the library of the 1980s is gone and will never return. This means that educational experiences that date from the '80s or earlier are largely irrelevant. To continue the watery analogy, the LIS professionals who have not identified the weaknesses in their knowledge and skill sets may be caught without their life jackets. Those who keep a sharp weather eye on the LIS horizon and continually adjust their course to avoid the dangerous shoals will reach port safely.

NOTE

1. "Planning for 2015: The Recent History and Future Supply of Librarians," *American Library Association,* June 2009, www.ala.org/ala/research/librarystaffstats/recruitment/Librarians_supply_demog_analys.pdf.

RESOURCES

Boone, T. "Ensuring the Visibility of Librarians." *Information Outlook* 15, no. 1 (January/February 2011): 10–11.

Fedeczko, J. L. "Library Jobs in Flux." *Illinois Library Association Reporter* 29, no. 2 (April 2011): 22, inside back cover.

Glasser, S., et al. "When Jobs Disappear: The Staffing Implications of the Elimination of Print Serials Management Tasks" [part of special issue: "An Oasis in Shifting Sands: NASIG at 25"]. *Serials Librarian* 60, no. 1–4 (January/June 2011): 109–13.

Goodman, E. "Looking for Opportunities—Backed by Transferable Skills." *CILIP Update* (February 2011): 46–47.

Janusz, T. "I've Signed Up on LinkedIn. What's Next?" *Key Words* 19, no. 2 (April/June 2011): 57–58.

Kumar, B. "Employability of Library and Information Science Graduates: Competencies Expected versus Taught—A Case Study." *DESIDOC Journal of Library & Information Technology* 30, no. 5 (September 2010): 74–82.

"Role Changing for Librarians in the New Information Technology Era." *New Library World* 112, no. 7/8 (August 2011): 321–33.

7 SURVIVAL STRATEGIES FOR PUBLIC LIBRARIES

Much of this book focuses on technology and its impact on tomorrow's library. For example, e-books and streamed video content will alter the library's focus, reducing the importance of lending print and non-print materials. The public, like the prime minister quoted below, increasingly views library success in terms of public access to technology. There is no question that responding to and taking ownership of technological change is absolutely essential if we are to have a rosy future. However, this chapter about public libraries is not about technology; it is about people. The technology revolutions of the past few decades have made it clear that public libraries are especially good at adapting to change. Early on, they saw the importance of public Internet access and incorporated it into their mission. They have usually embraced new technology that met the needs of their patrons. Much of the current difficulty surrounding e-books is the fault of publishers and distributors, not libraries. However, the future well-being of our libraries will have much more to do with people than with things. Our society is changing rapidly and, as has always been the case with public libraries, understanding those changes is absolutely central to our survival as a healthy and vigorous institution.

LIBRARIES IN RECESSION

There is no question that the worldwide economic recession has had a very destabilizing effect on libraries. As I write, Britain's public libraries are facing an especially disturbing future. Approximately 400 libraries are targeted for closure and there is talk of adding others to the list. I can't peer into the future, but I can make an educated guess that some of these libraries will be saved because of public protest. One community checked out every book in the library, leaving completely empty shelves. Public personalities have sent letters objecting to the plan, and many local residents are defending their libraries. Some of these efforts should bear fruit but, nevertheless, many libraries will close their doors. Those of us on the other side of the Atlantic will understand the enormity of this crisis if we remember that the U.S. population is about five times that of Britain. This means that proportionately, a similar crisis here would mean the extinction of 2,000 public libraries, a tragedy of almost unbelievable proportions.

We in the library profession are inclined to think that the public library has been so fully accepted into our culture that no legislative body would ever dream of destroying the institution itself. Of course, they might expect us to operate with inadequate budgets, reduced services, and otherwise make do with "stone soup." However, in our presence at least, legislators have always paid tribute to the essential nature of the library. A loss of 400 libraries in Britain or 2,000 in the United States means far more than some uncomfortable belt tightening. It is a statement asserting that libraries are unnecessary luxuries; communities may enjoy their libraries during good times but can get along perfectly well without them if necessary.

The well-known American librarian Walt Crawford has been researching U.S. library closures, and he's convinced that things are not as bad as we feared.[1] Crawford can find no evidence of the huge number of library closures predicted earlier in the recession. At this writing, however, things are not improving in the public sector. While businesses are making a slow comeback, state and local government fiscal crises keep getting worse, rather than better. I hate to be a naysayer but it is possible that the worst is yet to come. Whatever the specific number of libraries closed, library positions eliminated, or library budgets slashed to the bone, libraries are facing perhaps the most alarming period in recent history.

Britain's Crisis

Prime Minister David Cameron made it clear that he thought it was the libraries' own fault that they had to close. "We all know a truth about libraries, which is those that will succeed are the ones when they wake up to the world of new technology, of the Internet and everything else, and investment goes in. That is what needs to happen." Poor syntax aside, Cameron's statement leads one to think that he hasn't set foot in a library for a long time and has little knowledge of modern British libraries. Of course, such a statement was not allowed to stand unchallenged. Labour Party leader Ed Miliband responded with "Only this prime minister could blame the libraries for closing."[2]

It can't be assumed that this is a crisis that affects only Britain. In the United States, fiscal conservatives like members of the Tea Party Movement have made similarly negative statements but, so far, they have not been accepted by the majority. I think, however, that Cameron may speak for a rather large part of the population on both sides of the Atlantic and we need to understand the assumptions behind his remarks. First, of course, is the assumption that libraries have become irrelevant and that attitude is based, to a considerable extent, on the further assumption that the printed book is dead. Libraries are not yet associated with the circulation of e-books, so this creates a huge hole in the public perception of the library's role. As we discussed earlier, e-book publishers have not been friendly to libraries and getting a foothold in this area has been difficult.

Libraries Are More Than Technology Centers

Next is Cameron's reference to technology. It is doubtful that he is referring to the library OPAC or RFID system. What he means is public access to the Internet. This is a service that has penetrated the public consciousness. "Need to use a computer? Go to the library." For Cameron, it seems to be our only claim to relevance. Almost all of us would agree that Internet access is an important service but it doesn't stand alone. It is integral to our mission to meet the information needs of our communities. Of course, we want our legislators to be aware of our public computers and Wi-Fi access, so it tends to be the subject of much of the publicity we disseminate to the community.

If David Cameron's view is shared by a large part of the population, the library's reputation as a populist technology center has come with a price. Even though they are popular with very diverse users, it is widely assumed that our computers and network access are used only by the poor. In working with a variety of decision-makers, I've come to the conclusion this is not a good thing. Though they feel obligated to provide services to the poor, it is taxpaying, voting, middle-class people like themselves who elected officials have constantly in mind. For example, I recall a comment completely unrelated to libraries that was made at a city council meeting. It was being argued by one member of the council that no one used a particular service. When questioned, the speaker qualified his statement. What he really meant was that middle-class people didn't use the service, and he may even have meant that he himself didn't use it. It turned out that the service was actually used quite heavily and the city councilman made his statement without any solid evidence to the contrary. However, this particular service might almost have been wrapped in a cloak of invisibility because of the population served.

Serving the Whole Community

Service to the disadvantaged must always be a central part of the library's mission, but being associated only with this group may be contributing to a legislative perception of the library as irrelevant. Throughout their history, libraries have played an important role in turning "have nots" into "haves." For example, many nineteenth- and early twentieth-century immigrants learned to read and write English and prepare for citizenship in the public library. The unemployed flocked to libraries during the Great Depression to occupy their time, educate themselves, and become more employable. But it should not be forgotten that middle- and upper-class women have always checked out best sellers and brought their children to the library. Customers at every economic level have come to the library to find help and support in dealing with the challenges they face in their lives. For example, they have always turned to the library for books about coping with child rearing, substance abuse, illness, and death.

In recent years, we have been especially successful in developing services for the disadvantaged. For example, DVD circulation and public computers have attracted large numbers of disadvantaged community residents who cannot afford to own personal computers, subscribe to Netflix, or patronize video stores. Once they become comfortable using the library, they may discover other library materials. We have long wanted to do a better job of reaching this population and find opportunities to improve the quality of their lives.

Serving the Middle Class

However, we must not lose those more affluent voters, and the trend away from printed books may jeopardize our long-standing relationship. It is this group who are buying e-readers in large numbers. One cannot overestimate the appeal of discovering an interesting book and downloading it in less than a minute. When these patrons compare such instant gratification with the inconvenience of getting on a list and waiting weeks or months for a library book to become available, libraries lose. Popular digital books and other materials must become widely available in libraries immediately. There is no time to waste. The speed at which e-books and e-book readers are taking over the market is truly staggering and it must serve as our call to action. The cost of providing every item to every borrower instantaneously will always be prohibitive, but we must learn to compete in this brave new digital world. None of our customers wants to waste money, and if we can provide for most of their needs most of the time, they will continue to use our services and advocate for us.

Understanding Our Communities

Despite the crisis in Britain, I feel somewhat confident in predicting a fairly rosy future for public libraries if they continue to connect with their communities and remain very, very flexible. In general, public libraries have done a better job than most institutions when it comes to taking the pulse of contemporary society. Successful libraries have become excellent listeners. They remain connected to their customers, networking during checkout, noticing circulation trends, and experimenting constantly with programs and services. An early twentieth-century librarian would have difficulty recognizing today's public libraries because externally, they have undergone such extraordinary changes. The public library has always sought to identify gaps in community services and opportunities for enriching people's lives. It's a formula that can survive most futurist scenarios.

Any library staff could probably write their own book about population trends in their own communities. For example, they're aware that the first customers to arrive each morning are retired men. They quickly fill every lounge chair in the current periodicals area and spend thirty minutes to an hour reading newspapers and sometimes popular magazines. The men rarely speak to one another, yet they seem to appreciate the companionship provided by the group. Knowing this, savvy libraries furnish these areas with comfortable lounge chairs, not sofas. Because the library staff takes the time to chat with their "regulars," they understand the role the library plays in their lives. For example, men who have spent their entire adult life getting up early and going to work continue to need a similar routine. Unlike earlier generations, they are less likely to belong to men's social clubs like the Elks, Masons, or American Legion. Longer life expectancies mean they can expect many healthy years beyond the traditional retirement age, but they need to fill those years with interesting activities. The staff makes sure there are ample newspapers, and they experiment with other ways to satisfy the needs of this particular group. They might display sports, hobby, and travel materials nearby, noting which ones are most popular. Similarly, they might experiment with a program on fishing, golf, or investing scheduled for early in the day. Some libraries have located cafés with small tables and comfortable chairs (not the soda fountain variety) adjacent to the periodical area because nothing goes with a newspaper quite as well as a cup of coffee.

RESPONDING TO CHANGE

Local history is an interest of mine and I enjoy reading about the pioneers who settled my small western town. Life was extraordinarily hard then and yet every man seemed to belong to half a dozen social clubs and undertook multiple civic responsibilities. I have no idea where they found the time but women were just as active. They held frequent quilting bees, hosted theatrical and musical evenings, formed literary societies, and engaged in a variety of activities intended to civilize the Wild West while still managing to get the cow milked and the butter churned. Compared to their forefathers and mothers, some of today's community members have a great deal more time on their hands. In recent years, public libraries have become extraordinarily adept at finding ways to fill that time with both educational and recreational experiences. Some demographic groups, however, have more time than others. For example, unstable economic conditions have resulted in more people working two jobs. People in the thirty-to-fifty age group may be juggling child rearing with long hours at work, making payments on the mortgage, paying for children's braces, and repairing the damage to their retirement accounts. For them, the library may mean only a quick detour from their busy day, perhaps stopping in after work to pick up a movie or a light novel to read before bed. We will probably not see much of this group until their lives calm down somewhat, although we will see quite a lot of their children and teenagers.

Lifestyle Changes

On the other hand, we see a lot of the single people in our communities and will probably be seeing more in the next few years. The number of one-person households has been increasing steadily. In 2005, for the first time, unmarried households became the majority of all households in the United States. The proportion of one-person households increased 10 percent between 1970 and 2007 from 17 percent to 27 percent. This may mean that fewer people are engaged in family activities and are less likely to spend time at home. The local public library can be a welcoming place for people who live alone, providing comfortable social interaction, interesting things to do, and a place to just "hang out."

When you come to think about it, where else can you go almost any time, any day without spending money, without being invited, without making an appointment or reservation, and without extensive preparation? If we compare the library to the mall, the library will usually score many more points. Although the mall may provide a pleasant, brightly lit public space somewhat similar to the library, it does so for a specific purpose: encouraging people to spend money. The library, on the other hand, encourages people to simply be themselves and pursue their own interests while asking little in return.

Baby Boomers and the Library

Certainly one of the most interesting opportunities presently available to public libraries is the retirement of baby boomers from the workforce. As we all know, the boomers are the post–World War II generation born between roughly 1946 and 1957. They comprise the largest population group in the United States. Other countries including Canada and Australia experienced similar population growth during those years. Since seniors are among the library's most regular customers, boomer retirements offer the possibility of many more people using the library. However, that's not all there is to it. Boomers are different from the generations that came before them. As a group, they possess characteristics that portend a different post-retirement lifestyle from their predecessors.

Boomers Are Unique

First of all, boomers are generally better educated, being the first generation to enjoy the huge expansion in public higher education. In their youth, thousands of new colleges and universities came into existence. Boomers came of age when Americans were enjoying a period of affluence and many had the resources to prepare themselves for whichever career they cared to pursue. To help them on their way, student loans became widely available, and so they entered the adult world with material and intellectual resources that were not available to earlier generations. Because of this "head start," boomers enjoyed greater affluence than previous generations and they had opportunities to pursue a wide variety of interests and hobbies that they can enjoy in retirement. It remains to be seen how much the current economic recession has impacted their incomes, but the financial head start they have enjoyed will still give them an advantage over less affluent generations.

Boomers Changed the World

Technology was also experiencing rapid growth during boomers' formative years, and it was not long before personal computers made their appearance. Thus, boomers are the first generation to use computers during much of their work lives and to arrive at retirement age with technical skills. Boomers led the social revolution of the 1960s and '70s, breaking away from the traditional ways of their parents and exploring a variety of other lifestyles. They arrived in a world that was closely tied to the past, and they created much of the world we have today. For example, women moved into the workforce in large numbers and they no longer assumed that they would become full-time homemakers when they married. Women of this generation have become professionals and executives, never achieving salary parity with men but nevertheless building nest eggs of their own, independent of their husband's income. Divorce also became more common, and larger numbers of both men and women are facing retirement as single individuals. Thus dating and remarriage are common. Boomers were the first generation to come out of the closet in substantial numbers, so they will bring their alternative lifestyles to retirement.

In fact, boomers are fully developed, highly individualistic, and independently minded individuals who will very likely revolutionize the retirement experience, just as they have been responsible for other revolutions. Late middle age is unlikely to turn them into people like their parents or make them less hungry for new experiences. Since they are also healthier than earlier generations, they will pursue more active lifestyles for many years to come. In many ways, a sixty-year-old boomer is physically more like fifty-year-olds of the past and their brains are similarly youthful. Their educational experiences have prepared them for cultural and intellectual pursuits that they will continue to enjoy well into old age.

Boomers and Successful Libraries

What will this mean to libraries? Boomers are both voracious consumers and seekers of information. They expect more from life than did their parents and they want it right away. They are less likely to accept things as they are and as members of the "Vietnam generation," they tend to respond negatively to authoritarian establishments and decisions. Boomers have spent their lives gathering, consuming, and responding to information in a way that earlier generations could never have imagined. While earlier generations saw themselves as slowing down in retirement and adopting a more laid-back lifestyle, most boomers are simply planning to move on from one kind of activity to another. When most librarians think of their older customers, they think book groups and cozy mystery novels, and volunteers willing to bake cookies for library receptions and perform rather boring library tasks to keep themselves busy. If we allow ourselves to view boomers in this same light, we will do a terrible disservice both to the boomers themselves and to our libraries.

When viewed strictly from the perspective of the library's own need to survive and prosper, service to boomers may offer our best and brightest hope. Because boomers are not accustomed to taking no for an answer, they have a long history of working with and against government agencies to get what they want. If they want the library to be financially stable, then they have the ability to make it happen. However, to willingly use these talents in support of the library, they must believe that their library plays an essential role in their lives.

Boomers May Not Be Library Users

It's likely that this was not the case during their working years. Of course, when their children were young, they probably visited the library regularly. But as the years passed, they may have found the library's hours to be incompatible with their own schedules. Some with long commutes may have gotten into the habit of checking out audiobooks, but getting them back on time became difficult. Library schedules are built around normal business hours, and remembering which nights the library closes early can discourage all but the most dedicated users. Thus, when that became a bother, they turned to Amazon. Online shopping fit well with their busy lives and so they became accustomed to purchasing other materials they once borrowed from the library, like thrillers and cozies, to help them relax at the end of their long day.

This probably means that boomers arriving at retirement may not be dedicated library supporters. Instead, they will go through an initial period of discovering what they want to do with their time, what groups they want to become part of, and which activities they will focus their passion and commitment on. On the one hand, these are people who already have well-developed interests. On the other hand, they have spent their work lives constantly rushing from task to task and from place to place. Since these are obviously not people who plan to spend the next twenty years in a rocking chair or even in a chaise longue at the beach, it is almost inevitable that they will quickly find themselves with time on their hands. They are going to be spending some time reshaping their lives and it is during these "teachable moments" that the library can make itself felt.

A Second Home for Boomers

In talking with librarians who have been successful in developing a strong base of boomer support, I've discovered that they share essentially the same strategy. As one put it, "Boomers need to be underfoot. You've got to give them plenty to do." Making boomers an integral part of the fabric of the library requires a clear focus and plenty of effort. Most boomers have more interesting things to do with their time than shelve books, and even the monthly Library Friends meeting may not especially interest them. They need activities to which they can devote the same energy and enthusiasm that they gave to their paid employment. Except it has to be more fun!

Some boomers have been counting the days until retirement and really want to just veg out for awhile. However, others feel a sense of emptiness in their lives when their days are not filled to the brim with the triumphs and crises of the workplace. One librarian decided she would capture new retirees as soon after their last day of work as possible. She began the twice-yearly tradition of an all-day retiree workshop, which she advertised widely. Her program had the look and feel of the conferences that retirees might have attended over the course of their careers. They always included stimulating sessions like money management (facilitated by a professional retirement planner) and community involvement (sometimes led by the local mayor), and she made sure speakers were genuinely worth hearing. Breakout sessions were also scheduled so participants could get to know each other and form new social groups. Of course, the librarian's ulterior motive was to boost the library and its programs so she made sure that each workshop generated some new library volunteers, friends of the library, and new recruits for other library groups.

However, the recession dealt the library a painful budget blow and some positions had to be eliminated. The librarian considered canceling the workshop because it required a lot of preparation, but then she had her inspiration. Carefully analyzing the job descriptions for the lost staff positions and reassigning some duties to other staff members, she set about creating new job descriptions for ten-hour-a-week positions. She designed them as real jobs with real qualifications, hours, and duties that were important to the successful operation of the library. At the workshop, she made her usual pitch for volunteers but also told the group the library had some job openings they might be interested in. Job descriptions were posted in the back of the room and the library was accepting applications. Though the jobs came with a few small perks, a paycheck was not among them. She was flabbergasted when she actually received applications from two highly qualified, retired business professionals.

Boomers Will Not Accept Boring

The library staff is often less than positive about working with volunteers. Although they may like being able to push off boring jobs, they may view volunteers as more trouble than they're worth. They may completely fail to consider what volunteers might actually enjoy doing or what talents volunteers bring to the job. This is a formula for disaster when it comes to working with boomers. The majority of library volunteers are women and, unlike earlier generations, boomer women have held down responsible jobs. They have been supervisors and decision-makers and resent being looked on as incapable of anything more than the most mindless tasks.

The librarian who designed the ten-hour positions described above understood that talented people willing to devote ten hours a week to the library expected something in return. They expected to be treated as respected members of a team whose worth was fully appreciated. Ego gratification is a basic need and boomers had become accustomed to meeting this need in the workplace. From day one, these new arrivals were called staff members, never volunteers. Their training was just as intensive and they were given the autonomy to make decisions and rule their small empires, just as other staff members ruled theirs. They were required to attend staff meetings and encouraged to participate in conferences and statewide meetings. Perhaps most important, they were not placed under the supervision of the library's least senior clerk but reported to the appropriate library supervisor.

Educating Boomers

Let's not, however, try to put every boomer to work. Boomers also require stimulating leisure activities, and like volunteer coordination, serving as social directors is not a job that library staff members usually enjoy. Perhaps more than any other group, boomers are interested in lifelong learning and they look to the library to help them fulfill this need. I was recently surprised in my own library when an academically inclined volunteer decided to offer a series of discussions on Homer's *Odyssey*. Although it sounded interesting, I couldn't imagine that the discussions would prove to be especially popular. Instead, the series became one of the library's most successful programs. From the discussion leader's point of view, there were actually too many participants, most of whom were boomers. Boomers enroll in formal continuing education programs in large numbers, but since they are not on a "career track," much of what is offered in colleges and universities is not really appropriate to their needs. Elder Hostel and other programs that combine education with recreation flourish, and that is exactly what libraries do best. Boomers are also interested in self-education and, of course, that is where the library collection is especially important. Finding ways to get boomers to the materials they want without long delays or complicated procedures will need to become a high priority. Once again, boomers are used to getting what they want. I do not mean this in a critical sense. They don't simply demand that others give them what they want, but are usually willing to put their own time and effort into making it happen. Understanding this character-istic is key to working effectively with boomers. They possess the skills to make the library more successful and the library possesses the resources to improve the quality of their lives, the building blocks for an unbeatable partnership.

Supporting Boomer Goals

Surveys indicate that many boomers hope to retire early. As a result of the eco-nomic recession, some have been able to achieve this goal through severance packages offered by employers motivated to get higher-salaried employees off the payroll. However, others have seen their retirement accounts plummet and want to continue working, at least part-time. Because they are still at an age when they could easily continue to work, many are attracted to the idea of start-ing a small business that can be run from home. In this case, they may depend on the library to provide basic business services like Internet access, printing, and photocopying. Even more important, they are depending on the library for how-to books on marketing, accounting, and other business secrets that can make them successful. Other boomers are not looking for paid employment but want to devote the same amount of time and talent to creative projects and nonprofit organizations.

Because boomers as a group are good at political action, libraries would do well to organize them. As lobbyists for the library, boomers excel. But how can they be convinced to come on board and devote themselves to furthering the library's goals? As the librarian quoted above put it, they need to be underfoot. One way of keeping them involved is to meet their needs for social interaction. They may be feeling lonely since they no longer spend time with colleagues at work. Book groups are, of course, ever popular but you may find it useful to test the waters to determine whether new opportunities are needed. Groups are usually successful when their members have a lot in common.

Adapting Library Programming to Meet Boomer Needs

If you look at your Library Friends association, for example, you will probably discover that members tend to be roughly the same age and friendships among members of the group are common. When new people come to a meeting, they will be more interested in whether they fit in than what the meeting is all about. They will notice immediately whether there are others like themselves.

If they feel out of place—in other words, if they are older or younger than other members, or if they are culturally or economically different—they will probably not become more involved in the group. We should never forget that our library customers turn to the library to meet their social needs just as much as their information needs.

Take a good look at your own library. Are there programming niches where boomers will feel at home? Is your Friends group so old and fusty that boomers will have little interest in joining? If that's the case, why not establish some groups specifically meant to attract boomers? A group for home business entrepreneurs might be just the ticket. Are retirees attracted to your area because of outdoor activities? Use this as the focus of some of your boomer programming. Have you met a boomer who was once a mover and shaker in the business world? What kind of group or program might she initiate? Just think! All that energy and vitality might be directed at making the library a more exciting place.

Male Boomers and the Library

So far, I have specifically mentioned men only in connection with the library's early morning newspaper klatch. Libraries have always found men to be tough nuts to crack. True, men are becoming increasingly aware of the importance of the library as place. Many will seek out a pleasant, inviting environment where they can get out of the house, enjoy the companionable feeling of being around other people, and be entertained by the library's materials. When they volunteer their services, though, we tend to make them beasts of burden, for example, lifting and carrying boxes that women may prefer to avoid. I was talking about this situation with a very creative library manager who has been more successful than most in bringing men into the library. She said that for the longest time, she'd choose a program topic specifically to entice male library users only to find that most of those attending were women. She decided that men seem to know this instinctively and shy away from all-female groups. Yet in this day and age, one simply can't post a "men only" sign on the library door.

After repeated failures to attract men, the library manager decided desperate measures were needed. Political correctness was going to have to take a hit. She prevailed upon a popular male patron to start a men's investment group that met biweekly for a brown-bag lunch. Every PR piece and every announcement specifically mentioned that it was a group for men. It got off to a rocky start and the manager received quite a bit of flak from her female colleagues, but she stuck to her guns. Today, the group is well established and has become something of a library institution. I'd like to think there were better and more democratic ways to bring men into the library and would love to hear about more successful programs.

THE CHALLENGE OF OLDER CHILDREN

In the United States, most mothers of school-age or older children work outside the home. The term *older* is difficult to define but in many areas, parents are not required to provide after-school care for children age nine and older. It is generally considered acceptable by law enforcement and family service agencies for those children to go home to an empty house or otherwise occupy their after-school hours without adult supervision. Yet it is generally agreed by educators and psychologists that children need some kind of supervision into their early teens. After-school enrichment activities provide more than just safety. They are important to children's personal development and emotional maturity.

Unsupervised Children

Parents may find themselves caught in the middle, worried about their children but unable to afford to continue to pay for child care. Sometimes low-income families are entitled to subsidized child care, but for many families the cost may be unacceptably high. The financial advantages of a two-income household may be almost totally wiped out by this expense, depending on the parents' incomes and the number of children needing care. In one-parent homes, the cost of child care may threaten the family's financial stability. Many parents reluctantly decide they cannot continue to pay for child care beyond the legal requirement. Besides, older children are likely to think child care is for babies and may demand their freedom. This means that our society is coping with an ever-growing population of unsupervised middle school and junior high children and the number of working mothers continues to rise.

Some schools are trying to adjust to the situation with latchkey programs, but for the most part, few community resources exist to meet the need. At the same time, many of the after-school activities in which children once participated have disappeared, or at least participation has sharply declined. For example, Little League participation has been declining since 1997. Similarly, Girl Scout membership has dropped precipitously since 2004. In some communities, the number of participants has dwindled to half its earlier number. The total membership in the Boy Scouts of America has declined by approximately 27 percent since 1997 and by about half since it peaked in 1972.[3] Although a variety of factors are responsible, fewer parents are available to serve as scout leaders and adult volunteers. Parents may be unable to provide transportation to music lessons or soccer practice.

Playgrounds which once attracted older children have removed equipment intended for their use because of liability issues. Most playgrounds now have charming play sets for toddlers and preschoolers, but those tall jungle gyms and the other large-scale equipment we remember from our own childhoods have been dismantled and sent to the scrap heap. Likewise, recreational facilities like skating rinks that attracted young people are disappearing in many communities. While funding may be available for programs serving at-risk youth, the average child in this age group is likely to have few options.

Older Children and Young Adults in the Library

Most parents are fully aware that their children need some supervision, as well as activities that occupy their time more productively than television. However, they often have few choices. Society has been changing so rapidly that the pace of change has outstripped the ability of society's institutions to keep up. Public libraries were among the first to become aware of the transformation. They have long been concerned about children being "dumped" at the library by parents, and they have experienced problems with such children becoming bored and disruptive. Parents may command their children to go directly to the library after school because it is the only place where they believe the children will be safe, but libraries have not always welcomed them. Today, however, libraries are coming to see service to middle school and junior high students as central to both their mission and their survival strategy. During hard times, few strategies are as effective as those that involve parents. True, working parents have little time, but they are highly motivated when their children's well-being is concerned.

Children who are left alone after school do not do as well academically as those who take part in after-school programs. Studies confirm that such programs help children in a wide variety of ways, including increased self-confidence and better social skills. Children who participate in after-school programs handle conflicts better. Establishing positive relationships with adults strengthens families and increases children's sense of responsibility.

YOUNG ADULT PROGRAMS

There seems to be little question that the library can make a huge difference in the lives of older children and teens. By forging a close relationship among young library users, their parents, and their library, it is possible to meet an important societal need and bring added strength to public libraries at a time when it is most needed. The democratic, nurturing environment of the library is ideally suited to helping young people define themselves as individuals and prepare themselves for the adult world. Library-sponsored homework centers have been shown to improve students' grades as well as their performance on standardized tests. Individualized help from caring adults is something that parents may be unable to provide, but it is essential to academic success. Older children can help tutor younger ones so children can learn from each other. Educational games and access to library computers make these centers more attractive to less dedicated young scholars, and arts and crafts workshops also provide variety. For children who lack adult role models, the individual attention that library homework centers provide may be the most valuable part of the program.

Unstructured Programs

Many public libraries opt for a less rigid approach that focuses on providing the kind of activities traditionally associated with scouting and teen clubs. The emphasis is on recreation and public service, rather than homework. Of course, the library's young adult (YA) collection plays an important role, but many activities take place outside the library. As I visit libraries, it seems to me that much of the real vitality in public libraries can be found in their YA programs. The enthusiasm of both the YA staff and group members is infectious, and I always find that I leave with a more positive view of the future. If these young adults continue to view their libraries as they do now as a central hub around which many of their most positive, enlightening, and enjoyable activities take place, they're going to be formidable library supporters in the future.

A concern that has been voiced about homework centers is that they often fail to attract the very students in greatest need. After all, homework centers may have more in common with the school environment than that of the library. If the child or teenager has been unsuccessful and dislikes school, he will not want to spend any more time than necessary in such an unpleasant environment. The successful YA librarians I've known have a touch of the evangelist in them. If there is any gospel that they preach it is one of freedom and independence. The library encourages young people to be themselves, to discover what they enjoy and where their talents lie. To use philosopher Joseph Campbell's words, YA programs encourage their members to "follow their bliss."

While homework centers are nearly always viewed in a positive light, some librarians wonder just how far they should go in providing experiences that might be considered peripheral to the library. Do they have a responsibility to fill older children's leisure hours? Some local governments also ask this question, perhaps frowning on what they consider unnecessary expenditures. How much staff time should be devoted to such activities? My own feeling is that successful young adult programs will be crucial to the public library's future success. Although homework centers are useful and sometimes well attended, I dislike the idea that we are corraling potentially disruptive students and keeping them from bothering our "real," that is, adult customers. If we truly want to involve this generation of young people in the library, we must treat them as rational human beings who are entitled to be taken seriously. If we simply intend to keep them out of our way, we will never fully appreciate the insights they have to offer. We will never understand the contributions that they can make to the library and the library to them. Some libraries have been very successful in merging the two kinds of programs, creating a YA experience that strikes a balance between work and fun. However, there are few successful library programs that are not, at least in part, created by the group we seek to serve. Nothing could be more true in the case of YA programming.

Looking into the Future

Many public librarians are feeling uneasy about their own job security, and some have reason to be afraid. However, I find it hard to believe that the public library as an institution is in danger. Nevertheless, especially in bad economic times, we must be mindful of the public image of libraries. It is absolutely necessary that they not be viewed as archaic remnants of the twentieth century or too closely identified with printed books. Public libraries possess a flexibility, a talent for reinventing themselves, that is not widely shared. Public libraries do not need printed books or CDs or DVDs or glossy magazines to survive and prosper. They do need imagination and the ability to respond to new situations. For as long as I can remember, we've talked about the library being the center of the community, but sometimes we were giving lip service to the goal without making much progress toward achieving it. Twenty-first-century libraries can't embrace any such halfway measures. This is no time to tread water.

NOTES

1. Walt Crawford, "Public Library Closures: On Not Dropping like Flies," *Cites & Insights: Crawford at Large* 12 (April 2012), http://citesandinsights.info/v12i3a.htm.

2. David Greene, "Britain Faces Closing the Book on Libraries," *NPR*, February 10, 2011, www.npr.org/2011/02/10/133656983/britain-faces-closing-thE-book-on-libraries.

3. "US: Boy Scouts in Fear of Going Out of Business," *Current.com,* December 27, 2008, http://current.com/news-and-politics/89658372_us-boy-scouts-in-fear-of-going-out-of-business.htm.

RESOURCES

Bell, S. "Fit Libraries Are Future-Proof." *American Libraries* 41, no. 10 (October 2010): 37–39.

Grant, C. "A Clear Call For Revolutionary, Not Evolutionary, Thinking in Librarianship." *Public Library Quarterly* 30, no. 2 (April/June 2011): 158–64.

Maicey, E., et al. "No Quick Wins in Future Libraries Work." *CILIP Update* (April 2011): 10–11.

Martel, M. D. "What Is the Future of Public Libraries?" *Argus* (Montreal, Quebec) 40, no. 1 (July 2011): 53.

8

SURVIVAL STRATEGIES FOR ACADEMIC LIBRARIES

A few years ago, I found myself interviewing a large number of academic librarians. I was collecting information for a book about academic libraries[1] and got a little carried away with my interviews. I could not begin to use all the material I gathered, but the experience proved immensely valuable. Among other insights, I came to the realization that large university libraries were experiencing greater challenges than perhaps any other type of library. Soon after the book went to press, I came upon an article in the journal *Inside Higher Education*[2] that to some extent sums up the views of a number of university administrators, and it sent cold chills down my spine. I make no claim that the article titled "Libraries of the Future" is any more accurate, insightful, or better written than many others. However, the thoughts expressed in it clearly warrant consideration.

A DISTURBING VIEW OF THE ACADEMIC LIBRARY

Daniel Greenstein was at that time vice provost for academic planning and programs at the University of California system. The article described him addressing a group of university librarians at Baruch College of the City University of New York. In describing the university library of the future, he pulled no punches. Tomorrow's university library will have a very small staff and will consist of little more than special collections and study areas. He went further to say that "we're already starting to see a move on the part of university libraries . . . to outsource virtually all the services [they have] developed and maintained over the years."[3] Although these trends have been in evidence for several years, the economic recession is causing university administrators to reevaluate the purpose and cost of their libraries. "There are national discussions about how and to what extent we can begin to collaborate institutionally to share the cost of storing and managing books . . . and, frankly, as funding needs to flow into other aspects of the academic program."[4]

In other words, university administrators like Greenstein are looking on those vast acres of book stacks and endless carpeted study areas as prime real estate. They see little point in maintaining book collections unless they are being used—now! They may be very concerned about the library's contribution to the world of scholarship, but they are in survival mode. That means they are focused on how the library supports the university's academic programs and how this function can be performed as cheaply as possible. While they support the library's obligation to preserve unique items directly connected to the university's history and programs, they are unwilling to pay millions of dollars annually to maintain vast collections of printed books or pay the salaries of staff members engaged in this task.

Greenstein's Apocalyptic Future

Decentralization was another component of Greenstein's vision of the future. He cited the growth of research data services that have come directly out of academic departments rather than evolving under library auspices. For example, the Cultural VR Lab at the University of California at Los Angeles and the Environmental Information Lab at the University of California at Santa Barbara have received considerable attention, but when administrators praise such projects, there can be an underlying assumption that the university library is a dinosaur incapable of such innovation.

Greenstein foresees increased outsourcing although he does not go into specifics. However, my own interviews indicated that many university administrators believe that most of the library's routine activities could be outsourced and a few would like to outsource the whole library in much the same way that many federal agencies have outsourced their library operations. A great deal of money, they believe, could be saved if both professional and paraprofessional library staff could appear or disappear with a signature on an outsourcing contract. This scenario is, of course, extreme. However, many university librarians will attest that they have had similar discussions with their own vice president or provost.

University Administrators View the Academic Library

What makes Greenstein different from most university administrators is that he has an LIS background and views the situation from the point of view of both the library and the larger academic institution. In 2010 he spoke at a conference in Manchester, England, "Survive or Thrive: Making the Most of Your Digital Content," and his comments are available online.[5] By that time, the state of California was in the throes of even greater financial turmoil, with the library budget plummeting faster than even Greenstein had predicted.

Few university administrators have been as upfront about the library's future. If questioned, most would express themselves more moderately, but some of Greenstein's points would inevitably enter the conversation. While community college and small private college administrators may or may not be supportive of their libraries, most have no plan to totally transform them or shrink them to a small fraction of their former size. Smaller libraries, of course, have problems of their own, but I think there is an urgent need for university librarians to prepare for hard times and consider the options available to them.

The Library's Point of View

Naturally the librarians attending the Greenstein presentation were not silent. "I think that's not a very accurate depiction of what I see happening at research libraries," Deborah Jakubs, vice provost for library affairs at Duke University, argued. "I see the exact opposite happening, that libraries are taking on new roles—[such as] working with faculty in introducing technology into teaching . . . there's a lot more intersection with libraries and faculty than he would lead you to believe."[6] I agreed with her comments completely but they failed to reassure me. Through my own interviews, I had discovered many of the kind of faculty-library interactions that she described. Academic librarians often possess extraordinary talents. They may have second master's degrees, know their way around the digital world, and possess a unique understanding of how information is created and disseminated. When academic departments come to know their true worth, they discover that collaborations can enhance their programs at little or no cost to themselves.

Partnering with Faculty

If you've been attending many conferences lately, you've probably noticed that a number of exciting library-initiated projects are making digital information resources more accessible to both university users and the scholarly world. Projects as diverse as those involving geospatial data, scientific preprints, medieval manuscripts, and grant applications are making important contributions to the dissemination of information. However, my interviews confirmed that there also seem to be a number of projects loudly touted at conferences that have limited value and don't seem to go anywhere.

Academic departments may view library partnerships more as nice extras than as integral to their academic programs. The collaborations may fall to pieces when teaching faculty no longer have time to participate. From the library's perspective, professional staff are expensive and funds are tight. How innovative can the library afford to be if the project means many staff hours devoted to a project that benefits only a single department or a single program within that department, or even a single instructor within that program? Library administrators must be prepared to defend every position and almost inevitably decision-makers ask why, when the university budget is in such distress, a staff member is being paid to do a job for which she was not hired. To overcome this obstacle, the project must represent a high library priority and must further the important goals of the library. In the past, many innovative projects were funded in large part by grants, but a lot of those opportunities have dried up. Much of the funding must now come from either the academic department or the library's regular operating budget. In addition, the project must be seen as more important than the one that's not moving forward because resources have been redirected.

Focusing on Future-Driven Projects

Innovative projects and collaborations with academic departments can pay off in terms of increased library visibility and a clearer sense of the library's mission. Such projects can help decision-makers realize that LIS professionals are multitalented treasures who can strengthen the university as a whole. They can demonstrate that the library has the flexibility to take on new responsibilities and thus become more valuable to the institution. However, quite a few of the projects I came across during my interviews did not achieve those goals. True, a number of librarians had friends or acquaintances on the faculty with whom they sometimes collaborated. But in general, I could not find many that brought together the technical and discipline-related skills needed or the commitment to pull off a complex, innovative project.

There is no question that some of these projects clearly point the way to effective twenty-first-century academic libraries, but other ventures were doomed from the start. They were really intended to serve as the basis for a thesis, conference presentation, or journal article. Once the article was written and the PowerPoint viewed, the project faded away. It was never integral to the library's goals and never viewed as important by other professional staff. Library administrators supported it to strengthen professional staff portfolios and support bids for tenure or permanent employment status. I couldn't help wondering if the Deborah Jakubs quoted above might be recalling stories of partnerships and innovative ventures that could be trotted out when useful but which were far from representative of academic libraries as a whole.

THE ACADEMIC LIBRARY'S HERITAGE

I apologize for opening this chapter on such a grim note. I do firmly believe that there is an important place for the academic library in the twenty-first century and I believe that Greenstein's somewhat apocalyptic view is overdrawn, extreme, and unlikely to become fully realized if the very talented academic librarians I know have their way. However, it is important that we take a close look at how academic libraries have gotten into their present predicament. All academic institutions have undergone extraordinary changes since the mid-twentieth century, and libraries have been affected as much if not more than other academic departments.

The Mid-Century View of Students

One of the most dramatic changes has been the transition away from the traditional view of students as powerless and groveling, drinking in the wisdom
of their elders. They were expected to accept what was dished out to them
because it was good for them. Just as children of that period were to be seen
but not heard, college students were also without rights and were expected to
jump through whatever hoops their instructors decreed. The students' rights
movement developed side by side with the civil rights movement, and by the
1970s student groups began to exert limited power on their campuses. Students
gained the right to challenge their grades and evaluate their instructors.

Academic libraries generally shared the institutional view of students. Students were expected to study and conduct their research in silence, sitting
on straight-back wooden chairs. They were expected to learn how to use the
totally counterintuitive card catalog and made to feel just a little stupid when
they failed to understand that names that began with "Mc" were filed as if they
were "Mac." They put up with these arcane rules and learned to find their way
around the library because they had to. There was no other choice if they were
to find the books and articles needed to write their twenty-page term papers.
There was a belief among librarians that students should learn to jump through
library hoops, just as they learned to jump through mathematical and literary
hoops. It was good for them. It was part of their education.

From Mausoleum to Modern Building

By the 1970s, when I emerged as a newly minted librarian, public libraries were
moving toward more patron-friendly services, but larger academic libraries had
changed little since the 1950s. I worked in a large mausoleum, a once stately
edifice that had been partitioned with ugly plywood, plastered with ancient
printed notices, and otherwise made as ugly as possible. Although the building
was outmoded, there was no need for it to be so ugly. It was simply a total dis-
regard for the comfort and aesthetic needs of the students who were forced to
spend much of their time there.

Soon, however, a handsome new library was built. Everyone commented on
how modern and efficient and interestingly designed it was. Yet from the students' point of view, it was no more welcoming or comfortable than the mausoleum. Whereas students in the old building had access to an ancient Coke
machine housed in a plywood partitioned corner, no food or drink was permitted
in the new library. Whereas students could bask in sunlight in the old building,
there were no windows in the new library. Chairs were no more comfortable and
the collection was no more logically organized, but the distance one walked to
find a book or a librarian had increased five-fold. In other words, the new library
was a somewhat more attractive warehouse space and students were expected to
appreciate their good fortune. Instead, they wasted hours and even days trying

to find materials. They were told materials were stored in off-site storage facilities and delivery would take three days. They were made to wait in long lines when other staff members could easily have been summoned to desk duty.

THE CHANGING ROLE OF THE LIBRARY

Most libraries have made huge strides since those bad old days and have become much more welcoming, student-friendly places. However, the question we must face at this moment in our history is whether that is enough. Libraries of the past were dealing with a student body that needed the library to be academically successful. Today, students may need the databases and other electronic resources made available through the library, but they do not need the library building. If, ultimately, they decide they don't wish to spend time in our buildings, we can be sure those buildings will be repurposed by our academic institutions. Space is always at a premium. Most library space is wonderfully open and generic. This means that the cost of transforming it into classrooms and offices is relatively low.

Administrators have always complained that we house our collections in choice, climate-controlled, expensively carpeted and decorated areas when they might just as well be warehoused at half the expense. With digital resources rapidly eclipsing print, this becomes an argument we can't win. We must clear out those acres of print materials that can be readily obtained elsewhere and use the space for people. We must also consider just how much space we wish to protect and that, of course, depends on the local political environment. A healthy, well-used library with lots of student services and classrooms located on the upper floors can be much more viable than an empty, moldering space of twice that size.

DOWNSIZING: A THREAT OR A SOLUTION?

As LIS professionals, we instinctively rebel against Greenstein's view of a shrunken academic library that is little more than a shadow of its former self. His view of the future library as little more than study space and special collections is so frightening that it almost seems to signal an end to academic libraries as we know them. However, the anxiety that such an apocalyptic vision generates should not blind us to the possible benefits of creating smaller but more effective libraries. The phrase "leaner and meaner" has been thrown around a great deal during the recession, but the idea may have some genuine value in planning future libraries.

The Demise of Departmental Libraries

The widespread move to centralize campus libraries during the 1970s brought much-needed economies of scale. More people had access to more resources and unnecessary duplication was minimized. However, the transformation brought with it an unexpected downside. Departmental libraries, housed adjacent to faculty offices and student classrooms, were integrally connected to and involved with their users. They were part of the teaching/learning community in a way that is very difficult to achieve when resources and staff are integrated into a central, multidisciplinary library. Central libraries can become islands, separate from the rest of the academic community. They may become so self-absorbed that they are no longer able to listen. They function as single large administrative units that communicate with other administrative units and no longer have a daily, direct connection to students and faculty.

Decentralizing the Library

As pressure mounts to use library space for nonlibrary purposes, perhaps the library might take a leadership role in the process by bringing academic departments into the library in a variety of ways and establishing library outposts within other academic departments. It may be possible to achieve the kind of communication and synergy that departmental libraries make possible while still enjoying the economies of centralization. In fact, automation and outsourcing can make it possible to put libraries in the middle of the action with no loss of efficiency. Greenstein describes the growth of academic research units that are in no way linked to the university library system. I certainly was not sitting at the meetings where those decisions were made, but I have been present while other, somewhat similar decisions were made.

Academic departments are always looking for opportunities to increase their share of available funding and power. Each would like to build an empire larger than those of competing departments. However, maintaining a separate research facility is extremely expensive and requires a huge commitment of staff time. If the library system could share the cost and provide assurances that the facility would really function as the department envisions (and not become a generic, plain vanilla library branch), most academic departments would leap at the opportunity. In general, however, libraries have been reluctant to share power. They have feared that powerful department heads would demand that library resources be diverted to their pet projects. Unquestionably, delicate negotiations are essential and each partner's rights and responsibilities must be spelled out in detail. However, we simply cannot stand by while others reinvent the library.

INFORMATION LITERACY

Dear to the hearts of academic librarians is their involvement in the academic process. Just as Jakubs immediately defended her profession by pointing to faculty-librarian partnerships, so most librarians consider their involvement in teaching and learning as a key focus. Among the more innovative areas of librarianship has been the information literacy movement, and it seems to be a niche that was made for us. The explosion of information has, indeed, been overwhelming and students do need to learn how to function in what can be a very confusing and even hostile environment. Undergraduates, especially, may lack the skills to differentiate reliable information from trash and even if they have identified useful information, sheer volume can prevent them from organizing it effectively. Thus, the information literacy movement can play a central role in making the transition to a vital and productive twenty-first-century library.

Information Literacy or Bibliographic Instruction?

As I mentioned earlier, I recall visiting an academic library and coming upon the open door of a library classroom where I overheard a librarian making a presentation about choosing reliable reference sources. As I passed, I heard her explaining the importance of selecting authoritative ones, specifically pointing out the advantages of *Britannica* over Wikipedia. I was reminded that I too had cautioned students against Wikipedia and encouraged them to use respected online sources like *Britannica* available only from the library's website. In those years, my idea of an authoritative source was one with roots planted firmly in the world of print. I looked on *Britannica* as representing authority because I and most of my colleagues grew up in a world where one rarely questioned authority. If a book came from a certain publisher, it could be considered trustworthy and suitable for the library's collection (assuming its subject matter was appropriate). If it were published by a less august press, further consideration was required, while certain other publishers were completely off-limits for purposes of collection development. There were few enough publishers and publications in our bibliographic universe that we could make such dogmatic pronouncements.

In a very short period of time, that bibliographic universe has exploded. A single publication like the *Encyclopaedia Britannica* can't possibly keep track of all the emerging fields of knowledge let alone stay abreast of important practition-ers and their contributions. It is no longer possible to assign the imprimatur of respectability to every document that's fit to read. No, Wikipedia is not authoritative in the same way as *Britannica* and future publications will also lack *Britannica*'s firm assurance that the important facts and ideas have been buttoned down, edited, corrected, and made fit for trusting readers. There is no shortage of authorities writing Wikipedia articles but, of course, there are plenty of people who wish to impose their own limited perspective on the rest of us. It's been fascinating to watch the gradual evolution of policies and procedures to maximize the role played by knowledgeable contributors and quickly identify contributors with other agendas, thereby creating an entire planet of potential Wikipedia reviewers.

Authority in the Twenty-First Century

Wikipedia is not as authoritative as *Britannica,* although some studies have found that Wikipedia actually has fewer errors per thousand words. However, that is not really the point. Wikipedia represents the twenty-first century, *Britannica* the nineteenth. Information has burst its authoritative chains. The quantity of information has grown exponentially and the library's customers no longer inhabit the world of *Britannica.* Their world is as complex and as lacking in authority as Wikipedia itself. Wikipedia was born in the computer age when everyone possessing Internet access can share every thought, every prejudice, every idea and research finding. First-world, twenty-first-century people no longer imagine that there is a publication with all the right answers. There's no question that students must challenge the reliability of their sources, but the old rules are no longer adequate. The academic librarian on whom I was eavesdropping was teaching not information literacy but old-fashioned bibliographic instruction—in other words, pretending to guide students through the complex realms of digital information resources with the skills developed specifically for printed books and journals.

Wikipedia also represents a different attitude toward information. During the heyday of *Britannica,* both students and working people looked up information only very occasionally. Since *Britannica* and other printed encyclopedias cost several hundred dollars, one usually had to go to the library to use them. Naturally, they quickly got out of date and though libraries might purchase the annual yearbook, these volumes tended to cover mainly world events, new scientific discoveries, and newly famous celebrities. The encyclopedia itself remained static, with each article providing exactly the same information. Even when the encyclopedia was revised, many articles remained unchanged because it was simply too costly and time-consuming to start from scratch. However, this wasn't a big problem because people really didn't depend on the encyclopedia for much of their information. The kind of information it contained was not needed on a daily basis. Some articles were actually interesting to read, but many were consulted only when school children wrote reports and term papers.

Overwhelming Demand for Information

By contrast, Wikipedia is consulted constantly. It includes information for almost every human endeavor whether it be recreational, academic, technical, or business-related. Not an hour ago, I myself searched it to find information about compact fluorescent light bulbs and the color rendering index. I feel like making a joke about how many librarians it takes to change a light bulb, but all kidding aside, even buying light bulbs has become more complicated, as has nearly every aspect of contemporary life. We consult Wikipedia with the expectation that the information has been revised within the past few months.

In a rapidly changing area like technology or world events, the information may have been revised last week or even yesterday. While people knew little about the world during the golden era of *Britannica,* most larger businesses are now international in scope, and the basic information that print encyclopedias provided about other cultures and other governments would be all but useless to the businessman who is flying to Jakarta or Singapore tomorrow morning. While *Britannica* users were mainly students and academics, Wikipedia is used daily by millions of people whose ordinary, everyday information needs have skyrocketed.

Information literacy should be one of the pillars on which future libraries are built, and it can serve as one of the most compelling arguments for hiring (and paying) highly trained LIS professionals. However, too often, we've seen academic libraries establish information literacy programs that sound exciting and innovative. On closer look, it turns out that perhaps only one or two librarians possess any real expertise and the others are going along for the ride. This majority has done no more than attend occasional conference presentations and add some trendy terms to their vocabularies. They are only slightly better equipped to navigate today's world of information than the students they teach. While faculty in academic disciplines are not permitted to teach classes unless they possess defined academic credentials, LIS professionals sometimes claim the right to participate in the instructional program without the qualifications of even the greenest graduate assistant. To survive in the twenty-first century, LIS professionals must be viewed as having expertise in something that matters to the academic world. If they claim to be information gurus, then they must possess valuable knowledge that they can share with the academic community.

THE ONLINE PRESENCE OF THE ACADEMIC LIBRARY

Central to the success of the academic library is its website. Ideally, the website should represent the library in cyberspace. It should be so useful and so attractive that it becomes a kind of virtual commons for the entire academic community. Not only should a wealth of electronic riches be made available there, but visitors should be enticed to enter the library's portal and then remain to sample resources and find other support for their academic and leisure pursuits. That most academic library websites do contain treasures is unquestionable. Much of the library budget goes toward subscription services accessed through the website that bring the world's scholarship within reach. However, convincing visitors that this is the case and that they will have an enjoyable and rewarding experience may be something of a stretch. This was confirmed in a report released by the Ithaka Group titled "Studies of Key Stakeholders in the Digital Transformation of Higher Education."[7] Academic librarians may imagine that the academic community accepts the library website as their main access point to scholarly materials. Perhaps because they are accustomed to providing printed materials that are available nowhere else but in the library, they imagine that their website is seen in the same way.

Limited Use of Library Websites

The Ithaka report found that while academic librarians considered the role of the library website as a gateway to scholarly information as "very important," faculty did not. They often found other ways to get to the content they needed, sometimes not even realizing that those needs could be met more easily through the library. Another report from Simon Inger Consulting titled "How Readers Navigate to Scholarly Content" reached similar conclusions.[8] The study found that users bookmark the library databases they use most often, avoiding the experience of navigating around the site. In fact, other studies have found that many faculty avoid the library website entirely by going directly to Google Scholar. LibQual surveys have made it even more clear that faculty are not satisfied with their libraries' websites and frequently choose not to visit them. Again, such findings often come as a surprise to academic librarians. They use the library's site for their own work-related and research needs and imagine that everyone else involved in scholarly activities does the same.

How Websites Evolve

Since universities provide the basic site template, librarians "fill in the blanks" with the help of a library technician in what they consider a straightforward way. They are either not aware that a body of expertise exists on website design or don't feel it is required for their project. On the other hand, both faculty and students routinely access websites designed by highly paid design professionals who realize that easy-to-use, intuitive websites do not just happen. Both librarians and technicians may add features as they notice them on other websites, but they rarely start over, and so websites become increasingly disorganized and cumbersome. When it becomes apparent that the academic community is not visiting the library website or when complaints are sufficiently numerous, libraries may hire a marketing firm to redesign the site. However, the result may be a disconnect between the LIS professionals who know what is important and the designer who knows how to make the site look good. The user may never come into focus and the difficulty in finding materials may never be fully understood. Site maintenance may once again become the responsibility of the staff and the site becomes even more confusing.

Information, Marketing, and Technology: Putting It All Together

As long as academic librarians understand little of what it takes to create a website, the problem will persist and the academic community will continue to avoid using the site. Effective websites only emerge from partnerships among LIS professionals, designers, and technicians. Unless librarians can express their needs in the language of the Web, they will just be talking to themselves. Take a look at your own website and consider how it might be improved. For example, you know what you want visitors to see first and the information they are most likely seeking. We frequently see essential links, unimportant links, and library news and events squeezed into text boxes and seemingly tossed about the home page at random. The eyes of visitors leap around the page and the central area may be wasted on links to rarely used resources. This is not the place to go into the details of website design, but suffice to say that academic libraries may be wasting perhaps their best opportunity to bring new customers to both the physical and virtual library.

Tooting Our Own Horn

In addition, we may fail to consider that an important function of the website is self-promotion. Of course, we want to get our users to the resources they need as quickly and efficiently as possible, but we also want them to know that they have the library to thank for these goodies. There is no question that marketing skills will be essential to the success of future academic libraries. We must find ways to let the academic community know what we do and how important our services are. Marketing tools are best wielded by people who understand what it is they are trying to market, another important reason for LIS professionals to be fully involved in the development of the library website.

Marketing our libraries effectively also means positioning our message in places where members of the academic community will see it. One interesting strategy for accomplishing this is to create online library outposts all around the college or university website. Small, highly individualized packets of research links can be added not only to departmental websites but to individual syllabi and other course materials. Swapping links with administrative and academic departmental sites is another good way to bring in visitors. Ideally, the library and its resources should pop up everywhere and in a way that boosts positive awareness of the library.

Twenty-First-Century Tools for the Twenty-First-Century Website

While I was interviewing academic librarians, I noticed that they were frequently engaged in preparing subject guides to be posted on their website. Looking over their shoulders, I was struck by how much their guides looked like the ones on hundreds of other academic library websites. They were holdovers from the old pathfinder days before electronic resources when one library's holdings and methods of organization were indeed quite different from other libraries. Most research is now conducted using electronic resources, and the package of electronic resources available in one library is not very different from the others. What is needed, instead, are individualized guides that connect library resources to specific research needs, and those guides, chock full of library links, will be better used if they are housed on appropriate departmental sites.

THE INFORMATION COMMONS

No matter what college or university campus you may be visiting, no matter how imposing the facility the library enjoys or how straitened the budget, the one place where you can be assured of finding students in relatively large numbers is the information commons. Sometimes called the learning commons, this is the technology hub of the library. Whatever technical resources the library makes available to its customers, they are more concentrated and somewhat more sophisticated in this area than anywhere else in the library, I use the phrase "relatively large numbers" because the term *information commons* may be trendier and more sophisticated than the actual library space that bears that name. Perhaps a decade ago, you could find an article about these exciting spaces in nearly every academic library journal. Funding was usually somewhat generous then and colleges and universities included a commons area in every construction project and renovation. Unfortunately, many of those high-tech spaces are looking dated, and seedy-tech may be a better description than high-tech.

Updating the Aging Commons

There's no question that students want their libraries to be technically sophisticated, and if you build it—in other words provide a well-designed, up-to-date, and well-staffed facility—they will come. But apart from their aging equipment, how are those early commons failing to achieve their goals and how can they become more relevant to today's students? It might be easier to begin with the students themselves and the ways their technology needs have changed. Back when the commons was a hot topic, most students depended on desktop computers. If adequate funds were available, the commons computers were loaded with some very powerful software programs that most students could not afford to purchase for themselves.

Students Use Technology Differently

Today's students are likely to bring their own computers with them, although they may still depend on the library's software and more up-to-date equipment. They may also use library computer equipment in conjunction with their smartphones, flash drives, and iPods. Students who need their own computers for taking notes, writing papers, and surfing the Web may be better off with lighter-weight netbooks and tablet computers like the iPad.

All of these computers need power, although some have longer battery life than others. In visiting a large number of information commons, I rarely find more than a handful of power outputs and inevitably, students are clustered around those few outlets, almost like scouts clustered around a campfire. In fact, I have seen a number of shiny new facilities designed within the past few years that also lack power outlets. Such spaces tend to have other deficiencies, like furniture design flaws that make the new high-tech equipment difficult or impossible to use. I think this occurs because designers plan their new high-tech facilities in a vacuum. They carefully read reviews, compare prices, and assemble an assortment of hardware and software that is popular with general users or specialized applications recommended by faculty. They may never, however, have used such a facility themselves.

Because it is not unusual to see students using two computers simultaneously, they need ways to transfer data from one machine to another. How will they do this without causing the library to run the risk of spreading viruses? Once again, the focus should be on people, not machines. Commons facilities often provide other equipment intended to interface with computers, like still and video digital cameras. How will they be used? How will they be protected from theft yet readily available when students have time to work on a project?

Ongoing Staff Training Is Essential

Too often, much of the equipment and software purchased for the commons goes unused because trained staff are not available to teach students how to use it or no one realizes it just isn't working. It is not unusual to see one or two students who enjoy exclusive use of what amounts to a $25,000 workstation just because no one is available to teach other students to use the sophisticated resource. Academic libraries may have bitten off more than they could chew in such situations. In other words, pressured by science faculty or the university IT department, they funded a state-of-the-art facility without really thinking about the trained staff needed to make hardware, software, peripherals, and people all work effectively together.

CLOUD COMPUTING

A recent trend called cloud computing is coming to the aid of libraries that find keeping up with today's tech trends is beyond the ability of limited staffs. The term *cloud* has long referred to the Internet, so cloud computing is naturally Internet computing. In other words, the software that students use is housed and maintained not on the library's computers but on servers in cyberspace owned by Internet service providers. That software may be free, the library may pay a subscription fee, or the library may be billed each time the software is used. Software loaded on the library's network is prone to a variety of problems and may need frequent attention to function as intended. Updates must be installed frequently, users can accidentally or deliberately alter settings, and viruses can make programs inoperable. Extensive troubleshooting by already overburdened staff may be needed if programs crash or develop performance problems.

Google

Google is a good example of a company that provides cloud-based software free of charge. Google Apps for Business includes a suite of basic productivity software similar to Microsoft Office but it is accessible over the Internet. This means that wherever students are working, whatever computer they happen to be using at the time, they can load their documents and continue their work wherever they left off. In fact, they needn't have a computer. A smartphone or iPod both have access to the Internet and so can probably access the same documents. Cloud-based statistics software is especially useful, and other programs are available to support practically every discipline. Science, engineering, and computer graphics programs are in heavy demand.

Advantages of Cloud Computing

However, libraries will generally find that it is not free software but more costly and sophisticated programs that best lend themselves to cloud computing. When you use a software program on the Internet, you start fresh every time. You may be copying files needed to make the program function and saving documents and data, but when you log out the program returns to the cloud. Staff are still necessary to assist users unfamiliar with the program, but they need not spend time maintaining the software. Cloud software, does, however, make some demands on the library's technical staff. Computers must be configured to automatically clear out all traces of cloud files and protect the privacy of users' data, so routine maintenance procedures may need to be revisited.

If fees for cloud-based software are calculated based on usage, the library may have the opportunity to offer students a wider variety of sophisticated programs at a lower cost than if a more limited selection were maintained locally. However, any software made available by the library must be supported by the library staff. In other words, though cloud-based software may mean less need for behind-the-scenes technical support, it will require that the commons staff be prepared to assist users with every program the library makes available. The absence of knowledgeable help is already a problem in many information commons facilities. It is not uncommon for staff to admit their ignorance and leave students to fend for themselves when they have a problem. If the number of available programs is expanded, user information needs will also increase and libraries must be prepared to meet that need. Otherwise, a service that should strengthen the library's credentials as a savvy twenty-first-century institution will, in the end, showcase its flaws.

As with so many other issues described in this book, the key to future success lies in a better understanding of both technology and what is taking place in the classroom. Too many academic librarians depend on a body of knowledge they assimilated thirty or more years ago. Librarians, on average, are older than members of other professions, and some studies indicate that academic librarians are among the most senior. There is absolutely no reason why an old dog can't learn new tricks. Like all the other libraries discussed in this book, academic libraries will be successful only if academic library staffs are fully trained to meet the demands of the new century. Whether requiring newly minted librarians to come equipped with better technical skills or experienced professionals to upgrade their qualifications regularly, up-to-date technical and information skills are essential if we are to chart a course to a stable and productive library future.

NOTES

1. Jeannette Woodward, *Creating the Customer-Driven Academic Library* (Chicago: American Library Association, 2008).

2. Steve Kolowich, "Libraries of the Future," *Inside Higher Education,* September 24, 2009, www.insidehighered.com/news/2009/09/24/libraries.

3. Ibid.

4. Ibid.

5. Daniel Greenstein, "Digital Libraries in a Networked World," presentation at the conference "Survive or Thrive: Making the Most of Your Digital Content," June 8–9, 2010, Manchester, U.K., http://vimeo.com/12635699.

6. Kolowich, "Libraries of the Future."

7. Ross Housewright and Roger Schonfeld, "Studies of Key Stakeholders in the Digital Transformation of Higher Education," *Ithaka Group,* August 18, 2008, www.ithaka.org/ithaka-s-r/research/Ithakas%202006%20Studies%20of%20Key%20Stakeholders%20in%20the%20Digital%20Transformation%20in%20Higher%20Education.pdf.

8. Simon Inger and Tracy Gardner, "How Readers Navigate to Scholarly Content," *Simon Inger Consulting,* 2008, www.sic.ox14.com/howreadersnavigatetoscholarlycontent.pdf.

RESOURCES

McDonald, J. "New Wine, New Wineskins." *College & Undergraduate Libraries* 18, no. 2/3 (April–September 2011): 136–49.

Stoffle, C. J., et al. "From Surviving to Thriving" [part of special issue, "Climbing Out of the Box: Repackaging Libraries for Survival"]. *Journal of Library Administration* 51, no. 1

(January 2011): 130–54.

Strothmann, M., et al. "Retaining Academic Librarians: By Chance or By Design?" *Library Management* 32, no. 3 (2011): 191–208.

Vallier, J. "Twenty-First Century Academic Media Center: Killer App or Chindogu?" [part of special issue, "Current Trends in Academic Media Collections and Services"]. *Library Trends* 58, no. 3 (Winter 2010): 378–90.

Vogh, B. S. "Opportunities and Challenges for Libraries: An Open Letter." *College & Undergraduate Libraries* 18, no. 1 (January/March 2011): 97–103.

9 SURVIVAL STRATEGIES FOR SCHOOL LIBRARIES

erhaps more than members of any other LIS profession, school media specialists are misunderstood and undervalued. Largely because of this fact, their future is also threatened. School libraries themselves have long faced challenges, but since the recession gained momentum, they have been taking an especially hard beating. In 2009, at a time when K–12 school enrollment was growing, almost all schools reported a decrease in funding for media centers and information resources, with per-student expenditures of just over $12. In the years that followed, the "great recession" further reduced budgets. At this writing, President Obama's proposed 2013 budget does not include funding for school libraries and eliminates $28.6 million that was earmarked for literacy programs under the Fund for Improvement of Education. In addition, the president consolidated the "Improving Literacy through School Libraries Program" with five other literacy programs, failing to provide a revenue stream for the new entity.

SCHOOL LIBRARIES AND THE RECESSION

For a number of years, fewer school libraries have been serving more students with fewer staff. The June 25, 2011, *New York Times* reported that Lancaster, Pennsylvania, had to eliminate 15 of the district's 20 librarians; the Salem-Keizer school district in Oregon was planning to eliminate the positions of all 48 elementary and middle school librarians under the then-current budget proposal; Illinois's School District 90 in the southern part of the state was running its libraries with parent volunteers; and half of the secondary schools in New York City were in violation of state regulations requiring a librarian on staff.[1] New York is one of a number of states, including Arkansas, Indiana, and Kentucky, that require every public school to employ a certified librarian. However, like New York, most states are finding ways to cut back, and the recent trend has been to rescind the regulations or find ways to work around them.

The School Administrator's View

In an interview with the *Times,* New York City's chief academic officer, Shael Polakow-Suransky, explained: "The dilemma that schools will face is whether to cut a teacher who has been working with kids all day long in a classroom or cut teachers who are working in a support capacity, like librarians." Many schools have already reduced administrative staff, frozen wages, defunded extracurricular activities, and cut other expenses once thought necessary to run a school system. School administrators also argue that technology has to some extent replaced both libraries and librarians, since it has become standard to equip classrooms with computers and e-readers so students can do research from their desks.

Of course, as librarians, we believe that the Internet can only be an effective research tool if students know how to use it. Evaluating and analyzing information are not skills that come naturally to students. As Nancy Everhart, president of the American Association of School Librarians, put it, the library is "the one place that every kid in the school can go to to learn the types of skills that will be expected of them when it's time to work with an iPad in class."[2]

AFTER THE RECESSION

At the present time, it is hard to predict whether the end of the recession will signal a resurgence in school libraries. Presumably, budgets will loosen somewhat and many positions will be reinstated, but it is impossible to know whether school media centers will return to glowing good health. That has a great deal to do with whether school librarians are able to make their case that students who lack access to a fully functional library staffed by a qualified librarian are denied an important part of their education. Will the profession retain enough innovators who are able to develop twenty-first-century programs and market both their libraries and their own professional strengths to decision-makers?

Like academic librarians, some school librarians got off to a good start when computers became common in libraries. We saw an opportunity to make computers part of our territory. Because we had long used computers for administrative functions, it was not difficult to extend our networks and add large numbers of student computers.

Media Specialists Left Behind

However, some librarians did not really approve of the Internet environment. They sometimes viewed it as a wild, uncivilized place where students were prone to waste their time and come across inaccurate information. They recommended reference sources that were essentially printed volumes migrated to the Web. They disapproved of information resources that were born in cyberspace and cautioned students to avoid them. Students were nearly always encouraged to use the fee-based databases that were expanded versions of familiar reference works (think Wilson's *Readers' Guide* and *Social Science Index* that respectively became Wilson's *Readers' Guide Full Text* and *Social Sciences Full Text*, etc.). Although periodical databases have been a boon to scholarship, other resources upon which libraries long depended often lacked technical sophistication and did not translate well to the online environment. Both students and teachers often felt that librarians were out of touch with the real world, and so some of the territory that they had early claimed gradually slipped away from them. Students who live in a world of Facebook, Google+, and Twitter have often become far more sophisticated in their ability to manipulate the medium to meet their needs than their librarian guides. Though students quickly become aware of the vast sea of online dross and become wary of it, they do indeed need help in locating the truly valuable resources that coexist with the debris.

If information professionals are to have a future in elementary and secondary schools, then they must have credibility with students and faculty. They must be viewed, to use a cliché, as Internet gurus who are completely comfortable in the online environment and possess enough expertise that they are worth listening to. Because such a huge chasm exists between the adult world and that of socially networked students, the Internet guru must understand what is really happening online. If today's students are to be successful in tomorrow's world, they must know how to defend themselves against identity theft and how to recognize a phishing scam when they encounter one. They must have a basic understanding of fair use and copyright. How do their download decisions impact artists, small businesses, and the many people who make their living in the music industry? How will these decisions affect their own access to music recordings in the future? Nearly every student faces hard decisions about their online social networks. They need to know why protecting their own personal privacy is important and why the personal information they post to the Internet today can come back to bite them tomorrow. Cyberbullying is yet another topic that information-literate students must understand and about which information professionals must become authorities. In other words, if we have, as we tell parents, teachers, and administrators, really embraced technology and made it our special contribution to the educational process, then we must take that responsibility seriously.

Leadership Roles for LIS Professionals

Looking around the world of school libraries and media centers, it is clear that there are many such gurus, and many LIS professionals are engaged in some remarkably innovative projects. School library literature is filled with examples of outstanding partnerships between librarians and classroom teachers that provide new opportunities for student success. Media specialists are spearheading projects that support the creative and educational goals of both teachers and students. Such projects may focus on creative use of webcams, animation,

Skype video calls to authors and other interesting people, filming and evaluating student work, podcasting lessons, and helping the school community better communicate using blogging applications like WordPress and Blogger. They are creating websites, setting up RSS feeds, uploading videos to YouTube, and creating an environment in which both students and faculty can communicate with one another through blogs, Twitter, Facebook, and Google+.

There is no question that exciting things are happening in school libraries, but LIS professionals, the innovators who are making such a difference in the school's educational program, may be selling themselves short. Many have failed to convince the educational community that they possess knowledge and skills that students vitally need. Nancy Everhart's insistence that students need school librarians more than ever may not ring true to decision-makers who view librarians as bound to the past.

TWO LIBRARIES, TWO WORLDS

So this in essence is the plight of school library media specialists, and many wonder if the situation has become desperate. I think it might be helpful if I illustrate the present situation by creating two imaginary school libraries. If I call the libraries *A* and *B*, both you and I are going to get mixed up and forget which library is which. Therefore, I think I'll invent the Lake View School Library and the Oceanside School Library. Living in dry Wyoming, I like those watery-sounding names.

Lake View School Library

Let's begin by describing the Lake View Elementary School Library. To be perfectly honest, it is a rather boring place. It is staffed by one full-time and two part-time library technicians. Several years ago when the budget was especially tight, the principal decided that the qualified media specialist was an unnecessary luxury. Why pay someone almost twice as much as a library aide to check out books, maintain order, and reset the student computers? That, of course, was not a fair description of the media specialist's job, but it was what the principal knew about. She actually thought of the whole library as an expensive luxury, taking up a lot of space that could be used more effectively. Perhaps when the county approved the renovation project, she might take some of the library's space for a much-needed classroom.

As far as the principal knew, the library was going along much as it always had. It opened on time, it added new books and media every year, and teachers brought their classes to visit from time to time. Of course, library visits didn't happen as often as in the past, but that was because computers were replacing books and other library materials. Soon the school might not even need a library. As it was, the area with the computer workstations was the only one that got much use. Since letting the media specialist go had worked so well, perhaps it might be possible to let one of those part-time aides go as well. After all, nothing much ever happened in the library. No one would probably notice.

Oceanside School Library

A few miles away we can find the Oceanside School. If I can take my mind off those gently breaking waves and the warm sun gleaming on the water (it's February as I write, so forgive me), I'll describe this library. A qualified media specialist directs it, and other staff members possess better-than-average academic qualifications. Unlike the Lake View Library, the staff was not only consulted but allowed to become thoroughly involved in the design of the library, so it is far different from the large study hall that the Lake View principal covets. The Oceanside staff were invited to participate because their principal already knew a great deal about what went on in the library and the faculty did too. That didn't just happen by accident. The media center director and her staff put quite a bit of time and effort into tooting their own horns. A monthly newsletter is sent regularly to the faculty and administration, as well as to the superintendent of the district.

Even when the media specialist was still employed at Lake View, he didn't feel he could spare the time for a newsletter or other library publicity; there was always too much to do. On the other hand, the Oceanside team knows that both their own jobs and the library's well-being depend on overcoming the archaic view of the library held by many of their colleagues. I use the word *colleagues* here because library staff members give the appearance of being educators. Even if they are not degreed media specialists, they are comfortable and competent in an academic institution. Classroom teachers see them as fellow faculty members, unlike the Lake View teachers who think of the library staff as clerks who might be equally at home behind the counter of the local supermarket. Staff members are good communicators. Like the director, they let faculty know what they do and why it's important. All LIS professionals are in the process of reinventing themselves. Of course, we've always had to do a certain amount of reinventing, but recent technology is forcing us to completely overhaul both our profession and our professional image to survive.

Addressing Our Image Problems

Our profession, however, has always had a very visible public image and many people think they know exactly what we do. They've seen librarians on sitcoms, in the funny papers, and in the movies. Whether Katherine Hepburn was playing a glamorous librarian or Batgirl was playing a bespectacled one, we have long been part of popular culture. The job titles of most professionals whose work involves computers and information are unfamiliar to the public. When they introduce themselves to laymen, they inevitably have to explain what they do. When we introduce ourselves as librarians, few people would think they needed an explanation. Unfortunately, the picture they have in their heads is usually an inaccurate one based on stereotypes that have persisted in our culture even though the work of librarians has undergone a total transformation. For this reason, perhaps our most effective survival strategy may simply be convincing both our colleagues and the general public that we are who we are.

Administrative Structure and the Media Center

But let's get back to the Oceanside School Library. Gradually, the media center has assumed responsibility for both instructional technology and instructional design. It has become a kind of umbrella department that provides a variety of services to both faculty and students. As many of you know, this achievement did not come easily. Many media specialists are veterans of territorial wars, and the outcomes have not always been to our liking. However, at Oceanside, the head media specialist possessed a gift for working collaboratively with other departments. The library gradually accepted more administrative duties, thus freeing technical staff and learning specialists to do what they really enjoyed doing. The Oceanside model doesn't work for every library. Personalities, of course, play a large role, and a wise media specialist is a realist. He understands the political environment in which the library must function and he makes choices that keep the library in the middle of the action. No matter what the administrative structure, an isolated library will inevitably lack political clout; it will not interact effectively with other departments and will not participate in school decision-making.

Technology and Comfort Come Together

At Oceanside the library and its staff are fully involved in the educational process. Colleagues would never think of them as merely the keepers of the books or the managers of the machines. Because IT and the library work seamlessly together, the library serves as the school's technology hub. This means that everyone who works there has strong technology skills. Web design, desktop publishing, webcam animation, podcasting, courseware development, video conferencing and production, instructional design, and networking are some of the areas of expertise possessed by the staff. Several collaborative activity spaces are available to students where they can work together on projects.

In addition, the library is a comfortable place to be. No matter whether the school building has been designed by sensitive, educationally savvy architects or by hacks who don't seem to understand the difference between a school building and a penitentiary, the library should be an oasis. The Oceanside Library invites students to visit before and after school or anytime they have a few free moments. Even windowless block walls can be made visually appealing, and full-spectrum fluorescent lamps can totally change the indoor environment, adding the warm glow of sunlight to the most institutional-feeling space. Above all, the library is comfortable. It is understood that students have many of the same needs as adults, like enjoying a sunny window and sitting in a comfortable chair. Though many prefer a somewhat noisy environment, others need quiet to concentrate, so the library is designed to meet both needs.

Planning Is Key

None of this has happened by accident. The director has always been aware of the library's potentially perilous place in the school bureaucracy and of his staff's vulnerability to budget cuts. When he arrived, he immediately performed a needs analysis and identified the problems the library and its staff were facing. Then, after he had had some time to better understand the needs, preferences, and prejudices of the school community, he worked with staff to develop a plan for a twenty-first-century library. The plan consisted of many small steps and each time a goal was achieved, the media specialist bragged about it. He made sure that the word got out to everyone through the student newspaper, the library newsletter, the participation of staff members in committees, workshops, in-service programs, and through all the school's informal communication channels.

The library's website and social networking pages are especially important channels of communication with the school community. These online presences both support the curriculum and provide recreational opportunities for students. Teachers can access the website during class, and students find the site so enjoyable that many use it as their computer's home page. Blogging is also encouraged and over time, it has become one of the chief ways that not only students but faculty share information with one another. Unsupervised blogs and websites can be a source of embarrassment to the school, and anti-social activity like bullying can thrive on a page carelessly maintained by inexperienced staff. No one in the library works in a vacuum. Technicians regularly revisit the sites they create and students understand that if they fail to follow acceptable use guidelines, they will lose access to one of their favorite activities.

Making Everyone Look Good

Savvy media specialists are fully aware that their bosses are often on the hot seat. The local print and broadcasting media seem to spend a great deal of their column space and air time criticizing the local school system. Decision-makers like principals, superintendents, and school board members take a lot of heat. These decision-makers desperately need to do their own bragging. They need sound bites when they are interviewed by local television stations and success stories ever ready for when they need to defend themselves and their schools. With the exception of high test scores, they may have difficulty amassing evidence that theirs are trendy, successful schools on the cutting edge of educational innovation. Class projects tend to follow established patterns, and awards, though reflecting positively on the school, tend to be bestowed only at the end of the school year. Technology achievements can make an effective case that the school is up-to-date and preparing students for the future. Stories of individual student achievement can be found more frequently in the library where it is easier for students to work independently than in the classroom.

Understanding that decision-makers may rarely enter the library, the media center director found a surprising number of ways to get the staff out of the library to work directly with faculty and the administration. However, this meant that extra preparation and planning had to go into making sure the library didn't suffer by their absence. Routine work got done, order was maintained, and the library always felt active but organized. This required juggling many tasks at the same time, and it was not uncommon for something to fall apart. However, all staff members fully understood their top priorities. They knew what absolutely could not fall apart and they had a plan for coping when one or more of their number was away for training or on vacation.

IS THERE AN IT MERGER IN YOUR LIBRARY'S FUTURE?

In the example above, the library staff had acquired a number of technology-related responsibilities. This brings up the subject of library-IT mergers that are becoming increasingly common. Both are support departments, closely related in many ways. Increasingly, decision-makers are considering the possibility of throwing the two together administratively and appointing a single department head. Is this a trend that should be supported by the LIS community or feared? In general, it can be assumed that most school librarians know a good deal about technology and most IT professionals know little about libraries. Perhaps I am overgeneralizing, but that has usually been my experience. In such a situation, the media specialist can probably make a strong case that she already possesses a good understanding of the roles and responsibilities of both departments and can effectively direct the activities of both. Combining the two can provide opportunities for innovative programs and sometimes economies of staffing. Encouraging crossover skills in both departments can result in more productive employees and an overall improvement in services.

The situation, however, is rarely as simple and straightforward as that. Ideally, the merger of the two departments should be a gradual process characterized by increasing cooperation and shared goals. Synergies develop over time and a united department gradually takes shape. If the motive behind the merger is entirely financial, such considerations may be ignored. What occurs is a battle for power. Two gladiators, the media specialist and the IT head, must fight it out to the death. The one who loses is either demoted to a nonsupervisory position or cut from the payroll. Gender bias continues to plague the educational system and too often, it is a deciding factor when choosing which gladiator will triumph. Although the situation is changing rapidly, media specialists are typically female and IT professionals are male. Since system-level decision-makers also tend to be male and few of them have any real understanding of the library, the outcome can be a foregone conclusion.

Savvy media specialists should consider getting to know as much about their IT departments as possible and experimenting with some joint projects. They might also begin thinking about whether a friendly merger is a possibility. If relations are strained, ask yourself why this is the case. Has your department been friendly and helpful or does it seem as if the IT department head has pointedly excluded or attempted to undermine the library? This is a place for excellent political skills. If you feel this is not a strength, find a mentor; in fact, find two mentors. Get to know a media specialist who has been responsible for a successful merger. Find out how she pulled it off. You might also want to know more about unsuccessful mergers and what exactly went wrong. In addition, it would be a good idea to better understand the interpersonal dynamics of your own school. How are decisions made and by whom? What role does the IT head play in school-wide decision-making?

THE SCHOOL LIBRARY AS PLACE

The trend in recent years has been to transform the school building into a fortress. Increased vandalism, school shootings like Columbine and other school violence, drug dealers who lurk near the playground, and teenage gangs have all conspired to focus school administrators and architects on safety rather than comfort or aesthetics. Both students and teachers who must spend most of their day in a large bare room without windows, bright colors, or comfortable furniture may discover that the only place where they can relax, unwind, and restore their energy for the work that lies ahead is the library. School libraries are much more attractive, inviting spaces than they used to be. They are appealing to the senses unlike any other area in the school.

Media specialists who spend their days in the pleasant library environment should be aware that the rest of the school community does not enjoy this luxury and may not even know that it is available to them. I'm convinced that enticing both teachers and their students to spend time in the library working on collaborative projects, using the Internet, or just reading a book can be an excellent survival strategy. We must use the tools and weapons we have at our disposal, and what we might call library ambience is surely one of the most powerful.

SURVIVAL STRATEGIES FOR LIS PROFESSIONALS

Overall, the future prospects for school librarians and media specialists are still hazy, full of financial, technological, and instructional unknowns. It is difficult to know whether a better economic situation will be able to reverse the downward spiral we are currently experiencing, and the future of LIS professionals in elementary schools is especially troubling. However, we possess a powerful weapon whose value cannot be overestimated: parents! There is no question that the parents who consistently involve themselves with their children's education do care about libraries. They want their children to become readers and view reading as one of the most important keys to future success. They express their concerns frequently and make sure school boards and school administrators know what they think. These parents are especially receptive if they understand that their children will suffer if the library suffers.

Communicating with Parents

What is more, these parents are visible and relatively easy to reach. However, most media specialists rarely attempt to communicate with them directly. Classroom teachers have the advantage of regular parent-teacher conferences to get to know one another. Librarians must find other ways to get their message across. And what is that message? Children who are avid readers become more successful students and that success carries over into their adult life. It is also true that children who are able to participate in a rich and stimulating school library program under the direction of LIS professionals are much more likely to become avid readers. In addition, active school library programs offer students opportunities for independent learning and creative problem-solving that may exist nowhere else in the school.

Parents must understand that the library's funding is directly related to their children's academic success, and we must not assume they understand this. Although it is not appropriate to lobby parents, there are many ways of bringing them into the library and making them aware of how its program impacts their children. A variety of programs, for example, a panel discussion bringing together reading and media specialists, can attract parents, and contests that feature evening award ceremonies can also be effective. A library newsletter can make the program more visible, and a number of libraries host an e-mail list or webpage specifically for parents featuring book reviews, links to good articles about reading, and announcements of library events.

Planning for Job Security

If you are currently working in a school, you may find yourself anxiously scanning the daily newspaper to discover what new threats are looming on your career horizon. On the one hand, you don't want to be caught unprepared, but the thought of waging a campaign in support of your position seems daunting. If your job is truly in jeopardy, you have what amount to three choices. The first, of course, is to continue as you have been, hoping that if you go on doing a good job, your contribution will be recognized and appreciated. The second option is to prepare for the worst. You may want to choose another profession that fits your skill set, analyze employment opportunities, and perhaps begin taking online courses to strengthen your credentials. The third choice is to put up an energetic fight, re-prioritize your duties, become a PR whiz, and find time to energize potential library supporters.

To be perfectly truthful, I'm not sure which of the three is the best choice. It depends largely on your specific situation. If your state or region has survived the recession with only minor damage, then perhaps the first choice is the right one for you. However, even under these more desirable conditions, this is still a risky decision. How do you know that your efforts will be noticed by decision-makers and your contributions will be fully appreciated? How do you know that major budget cuts aren't lurking around the corner? In my personal experience, staffing cuts are rarely expected. School personnel live in their own departmental cocoons and rarely know what's going on in the minds of budget-cutting school boards and administrators.

On the other hand, if your local government is deep in a real financial crisis, then you'd probably do best by strapping on your parachute. It may be that your situation is a perilous one and there is little you can do to stabilize or strengthen your position. You should be looking at other locales with more stable economies or other career paths that are less affected by the recession.

Perhaps the third choice might be considered the Goldilocks option. In other words, your environment is not too hot and not too cold, not in crisis but not doing terribly well. It's worth putting up a good fight because there's a reasonable chance that you can prevail. By mobilizing the resources available to you, it may be possible to make a difference both in your own personal security and the library's. Although I've considered each of these choices in isolation, the best alternative may be to hedge your bets and incorporate some elements of all three choices into your survival strategy. Of course, this could escalate into a 24-hour job, so you must choose your priorities carefully and consider where your strengths lie.

When peering into the future, we will inevitably lack objectivity. However, there are few organizations that can impact the twenty-first century as positively as the school library. While a school library that lacks the services of a media specialist can become little more than a room full of books and computers, LIS professionals can transform boring spaces into creative experiences. They can make a profound difference in the way future citizens will use information to make their world better.

NOTES

1. "In Lean Times, Schools Squeeze Out Librarians," *New York Times,* June 25, 2011, A17.
2. Ibid.

RESOURCES

Hough, M. "Libraries as iCentres: Helping Schools Face the Future." *School Library Monthly* 27, no. 7 (April 2011): 8–11.

"Imagining the Future of the School Library." *Design Share: Designing for the Future of Learning* (e-newsletter). July 2011. www.designshare.com/index.php/articles/school-library-future/.

Mardis, M. A. "A Big Vision Depends on a Long Memory: One Professor's Take on 21st-Century School Libraries." *School Library Monthly* 27, no. 6 (March 2011): 45–47.

Mondloch, B. "Libraries of the 21st Century." *School Library Monthly* 27, no. 7 (April 2011): 45–47.

Orlando, Demetri. "School Library of the Future, Now?" *Independent School Educators Network.* September 25, 2010. http://isenet.ning.com/forum/topics/school-library-of-the-future?xg_source=activity.

Pearson, Chris. "School Libraries 21C: Hosted by School Libraries and Information Literacy." 2011. http://schoollibraries21c.edublogs.org.

Peyton, Lindsay. "School Libraries Forecast a Digital Future." *Ultimate Conroe.* August 5, 2011. www.ultimateconroe.com/stories/238072-school-libraries-forecast-a-digital-future.

Purcell, M. "The Vision: Libraries of the Future." *Library Media Connection* 29, no. 4 (January/February 2011): 38–39.

CONCLUSION

Whether discussing the future of libraries or space travel, prognosticators have a bad habit of being wrong. There are always developments occurring quietly in the background, while the big splash that gets all the attention is just that—an attention grabber that quickly disappears. Librarians, like everyone else, are susceptible to media outlets constantly announcing the next big thing, the wave of the future. Just five years ago, I had no idea what a smartphone was and thought owning a cell phone meant I was hip to the latest technology. Now, it's hard to remember that I couldn't check my e-mail when I was on the road. I probably never gave it a thought, and the idea that half a billion people would carry on much of their social life at one particular website would have seemed ludicrous to me. How did I come to view my "Droid" almost as a part of my anatomy? Of course, futurists do get it right sometimes, so it's important to tune in and be aware of the pundits who make their predictions on the nightly news. However, observing your customers and their developing habits and interests may be more useful.

FOCUSING ON OUR CUSTOMERS

To gather information for my books, I interview a large number of librarians. Recently, we've been discussing the recession and the cuts in services that have become necessary. As librarians explained why they chose to cut in one area rather than another, I found that they were generally well aware of their users' needs and anxious to minimize the negative impact of the cuts. Nevertheless, I heard some use the words *should* and *shouldn't* frequently in reference to their users. For example, when considering limiting evening hours they might say "They should be able to get to the library earlier," or when defending the reduced technology budget, "They should be willing to wait for a computer to become available." Librarians have absolutely no right to decide how the library will fit into their customers' lives. Sure, children shouldn't play with the elevator and teenagers should remove their in-line skates before entering the library, and Mrs. Jones should use her cell phone in the area designated for this purpose. Without such basic rules, the library might become a dangerous and unpleasant place. Making judgments about the way people live their lives, however, is another matter entirely. In addition to being guilty of hubris when we exhibit such attitudes, we also lessen the likelihood that our libraries and our profession will move forward into an exciting, successful, and productive twenty-first century. When customers become dissatisfied and choose to spend their time elsewhere, we fail to realize it is partly our own fault and refuse to accept responsibility. Of course, we can't satisfy everyone and we must do a certain amount of triage. However, unless we listen to our customers and shape the library around their most pressing needs and wants, libraries and their "keepers" will become increasingly irrelevant.

Taking Stock of Our Assets

LIS professionals must become acute observers, asking questions and watching usage patterns closely. They must be on top of demographic changes, noticing how lifestyles are evolving in unexpected ways. How is the unemployment picture affecting library users and how are working people's schedules changing? What we have learned again and again over the years is that our communities will support their library only when it meets their needs. We have to recognize that when the library reduces its hours, it will inevitably lose some of its supporters. Such changes may be necessary, but to gloss over them with self-serving pronouncements about how customers should alter their schedules is inexcusable.

Earlier in this book, we discussed the increasing problem of older children whose mothers are working and who have few places to go. Of course, libraries cannot meet every societal need, but our ears should perk up when we come upon needs that dovetail with the library's mission and goals. Automatically assuming that someone else should deal with the problem is shortsighted and may hurt both the library and the children concerned. The challenges faced by our communities, businesses, and educational institutions came about as a result of a complex set of societal changes leading up to the present state of affairs. Whether or not these should have happened is irrelevant. The question is, how can the library respond?

Changing Neighborhoods

Most public library hours have changed little since the days when mothers were free to bring their children to the library during the day. Last year, I was visiting my daughter and we were out for a walk. She had taken time off from work for my visit, but no one else in her neighborhood seemed to be at home. We made jokes about the eerie "graveyard" feel, the absence of cars in the streets or residents in their yards. When we reached the local branch of the public library, the same sense of abandonment prevailed. Although the staff parking lot was occupied, indicating that the library was presumably open, not a car could be seen in the public lot. The library reflected the neighborhood of young families and working couples. By six, the streets and sidewalks would be bustling with activity but for now, the library might just as well close its doors. Academic libraries where evening and weekend programs have come to dominate the curriculum also need to rethink their priorities.

I know almost nothing about my daughter's branch library. It may have lots of successful programs of which I'm unaware or I may have hit an unusually slow day. However, it does not take a crystal ball to realize that others will notice that money spent on this library might be put to better use. I recently checked the library's website and discovered that Saturday hours have been shortened but weekday hours are unchanged. I can't help but wonder whether the branch manager thought that local residents "should" be able to visit the library on weekdays.

Reassessing Our Priorities

Again, I don't know about the choices that have been made in this particular library. However, in talking to many librarians, I have frequently been assured that it is not possible to provide innovative new services during the current economic crisis because staff resources are already being stretched too thin. When I inquire further, I learn that these librarians are beginning with the duties currently being performed by the library staff and assuming that new services would require additional staff time. In other words, they are automatically supposing that new services are less important than existing ones and staff duties are somehow carved in stone. Especially in libraries where senior staff have been performing similar duties for many years, no one ever stops and wonders what would happen if something just didn't get done.

Yet today's library is totally unlike the library at the time many of those tasks were added to job descriptions. Whole collections have disappeared, customers have ceased to use once-successful services, and computers have reduced the need for manual record-keeping. Most of us are familiar with zero-based budgeting that requires budget preparers to start from scratch. They must defend not just requested increases in funding but every current personnel and program expenditure. Perhaps we need to practice something like zero-based staff resource allocation. Every task a staff member performs is open to discussion. The task must result in more benefit to the library's customers than another task that isn't getting done. Every program must result in more benefit to the library's customers than a program that hasn't been implemented.

Libraries Stepping Up to the Plate

On the other hand, my interviews have allowed me to see some wonderfully effective libraries of all types. Of course, a stable budget is an important component of library success, but some of the librarians I've met have decided to take on the challenge of the recession to create new programs and services. Libraries in hard-hit, economically depressed cities sponsor job fairs, host coffee klatches for the unemployed, and sponsor swap meets where children's clothing is exchanged. In other communities, libraries reach out to improve the lives of seniors, young mothers, young children, working men, and minorities. As other community institutions and organizations flounder, these libraries grow stronger. As academic librarians see their reading rooms emptying out, they discover other social and academic needs that are not being met on their campuses. LIS information skills place our profession in a unique position to analyze trends in our community and respond to them. As long as these skills continue to inform our mission and goals, it's hard to believe that libraries will not have a vital role to play in the next hundred years.

INDEX

challenges of, 65–66
latchkey, 90
LIS types, 76
recession and, 125–126
survival strategies for, 91–93
unstructured types, 92–93
projects, future-driven, 97
public facilities, absence of, 56–57
public library strategies
Britain's crisis, 79–80
changes and, 82–88
community services and, 80–82
libraries in recession, 78–79
older children, 90–91
programs and, 91–93
technology centers and, 80
publishers, Amazon *vs.*, 22–23

R

Random House, 14
Reader (Sony), 8–9
ReadersFirst initiative, 17–18
realtime web, defined, 46
recession
outsourcing and, 33
school libraries and, 111
survival strategies of, 78–79
retrospective conversion, outsourcing, 32
revitalization suggestions, 66–67
RFID tags, outsourcing, 32

S

Schneier, Bruce, 16
school libraries
administrators and, 111–112
image of, 115–116
job security, 120–121
leadership roles in, 113–115
media specialists and, 112–113
parent communication and, 120
structure and, 116–119
security, importance of, 61
Simon & Schuster, 14
Slater, Charles, 16

social networking
commitment to, 49
customers and, 50–51
experiences with, 49–50
fans and followers, 51–52
language of, 52
multitasking and, 47–48
planning presence, 50
staff and, 52–53
students and, 46–47
society, changes in, 55–57
software types, 10–11
Sony Readers, 8–9
space considerations
companionship and, 62–63
environmental considerations, 64–67
individual preferences, 63–64
library experience as, 59–61
response to needs, 58–59
role of library, 57–58
societal changes, 55–57
staff and, 63
Spring Design Alex eReader, 9
staff
academic libraries and, 107
automation and, 38
library experience and, 63
outsourcing and, 33–34, 38–39
social networking and, 52–53
temporary, 32
training and, 107
staffless libraries, 40–41
strategies. *see* public library strategies
students
rights of, 98
technology use and, 106–107
subscription management, outsourcing, 32

T

technology, communication gap and, 73–74
technology centers, strategies of, 80
The Third Wave (Toffler), 1

titles, librarian, 73
Toffler, Alvin, 1
Twitter (social network), 46–53

U
unsupervised children, 90–91
use agreements, 16–17

V
Vernor v. Autodesk, 16

W
Watson, Thomas, 2
website *vs.* blog, 53

websites
    academic libraries and, 104–106
    design outsourcing, 32
Wikipedia (online encyclopedia), 45–46,
        101–102
Wolf, Maryanne, 6
WordPress, 53

Y
young adult programs, 91–92
YouTube (social media), 27

You may also be interested in

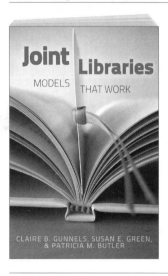

JOINT LIBRARIES
MODELS THAT WORK

Claire B. Gunnels, Susan E. Green, and Patricia M. Butler

Three founding faculty librarians of a joint-use college/public library discuss the factors that should go into evaluating when and where a joint library is suitable.

ISBN: 978-0-8389-1138-9
232 PAGES / 6" × 9"

WORKING IN THE VIRTUAL STACKS
LAURA TOWNSEND KANE ED.
ISBN: 978-0-8389-1103-7

A LIBRARIAN'S GUIDE TO AN UNCERTAIN JOB MARKET
JEANNETTE WOODWARD
ISBN: 978-0-8389-1105-1

HIRING, TRAINING, AND SUPERVISING LIBRARY SHELVERS
PATRICIA TUNSTALL
ISBN: 978-0-8389-1010-8

PUBLIC LIBRARIES GOING GREEN
KATHRYN MILLER
ISBN: 978-0-8389-1018-4

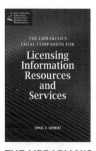

THE LIBRARIAN'S LEGAL COMPANION FOR LICENSING INFORMATION RESOURCES AND SERVICES
TOMAS A. LIPINSKI
ISBN: 978-1-5557-0610-4

COUNTDOWN TO A NEW LIBRARY, 2E
JEANNETTE WOODWARD
ISBN: 978-0-8389-1012-2

Order today at **alastore.ala.org** or **866-746-7252!**
ALA Store purchases fund advocacy, awareness, and accreditation programs for library professionals worldwide.